MAKING CHOICES

Making Choices

Practical Wisdom for
Everyday Moral Decisions

reread 22/10/11

Peter Kreeft

Servant Books
Ann Arbor, Michigan

Cover design by Steve Eames

Published by Servant Publications
P.O. Box 8617
Ann Arbor, Michigan 48107

Printed in the United States of America
ISBN 0-89283-638-5

00 01 02 03   16 15 14 13

Library of Congress Cataloging-in-Publication Data

Kreeft, Peter.
Making choices : practical wisdom for everyday moral
decisions / by Peter Kreeft.
       p.   cm.
   "A Redeemer book."
   ISBN 0-89283-638-5
   1. Christian ethics—Catholic authors. 2. Spiritual life-
Catholic authors. I. Title.
BJ1249.K774   1990
241—dc20   89-78401
                                                     CIP

Dedication

For Jake and Marge

Contents

Preface

THIS IS A BOOK ABOUT ETHICS, OR MORALITY. But it is different from most books on this subject.

Most books on ethics focus on controversial issues like war, capital punishment, or euthanasia, and try to resolve these issues by moral reasoning. In other words, most books offer the reader the fruits of the author's discernment, by which he applies principles to hard cases.

This book does not focus on that aspect of morality for three reasons. First, because controversial, hard cases are usually rare (abortion is a notable exception), and the average individual only very occasionally confronts such choices. The vast majority of our moral choices concern the old, ordinary, noncontroversial, forgotten truths that I have tried to recall and restore in this book.

Second, because I want to leave most particular discernments up to you, as God left it up to us. I cannot and will not be your conscience for you, especially on matters I am unsure of myself.

Third, and most importantly, because I wanted to call attention to those aspects of practical morality most forgotten and most needed in our immoral society: character building, principles, absolutes, the end and meaning of life, our society's blind spots, the source of power to practice moral ideals, and the need to be "counter-cultural" in our spiritual warfare. I think these are the most practical and most needed parts of morality today, not clever and controversial moral reasoning about specific, uncertain, currently fashionable issues.

So here is an old-fashioned book for you.

Part One

Problems: The Modern Moral Crisis

ONE

Our Immoral World: Are We More Barbaric Than Our Ancestors?

The times are never so bad that a good man cannot live in them.
—*St. Thomas More*

THE TIMES ARE BAD

The naive optimism of the sixties is dying because our civilization is dying. And our civilization is dying because its fundamental foundation and building block, the family, is dying.

Parents know today that it's a moral jungle out there. They fear for their children's safety, their survival, and their very souls. Body, soul, and spirit are all threatened; health, happiness, and holiness are very difficult to maintain.

A survey of high school principals in 1958 asked this question: What are the main problems among your students? The answer was:

1. not doing homework
2. not respecting property—*e g.*, throwing books

3. leaving lights on and doors and windows open
4. throwing spitballs in class
5. running through the halls

The same survey question was asked a mere thirty years (one generation) later, in 1988. The answers were startlingly different. Here are the main problems of today's high school students:

1. abortion
2. AIDS
3. rape
4. drugs
5. fear of violent death, murder, guns and knives in school.

Parents are no better off than kids. The family is falling like Humpty Dumpty, and all the king's horses and all the king's men haven't been able to put it back together again. And the family is the *only* place most people can learn life's single most important lesson, unselfish love.

Half of all American marriages end in divorce. *Most* kids have one parent or none at home, not two. Many marriages, even when they hold together, are full of tension, bitterness, resentment, and depression. Ann Landers asked married readers to respond to the question: If you had to do it over again, would you marry your spouse? She was astonished at the volume of the reply, and even more at the fact that over seventy-five percent of them said no. If half of all marriages end in divorce and three quarters of those that don't are unhappy, that means only one marriage in eight is a good one. Hey, kids, seven chances out of eight you're going to learn you can't find trust, love, security, or happiness anywhere, not even in your own home. What kind of a society can be built out of those building blocks?

Fidelity in marriage and chastity outside it are no longer the norm, but the exception. The majority of today's unmarried teenagers have lost their virginity; in fact, many teenagers no longer understand what that word even means, literally. Sex is now so common that the thrill is gone, so (according to another survey) the biggest thrill in life for most women in America, especially teenagers, is not sex but *shopping!*

Greed for *things* tops even lust for sex. Our whole economic system is based on greed. This is so taken for granted that we hardly ever think of it. More people—young, middle-aged, and old alike—worry more about money than anything else, even death. Political candidates, at every level of government, emphasize their economic policies as the number-one reason for voting for them. It's the only subject no candidate can ever possibly ignore and still hope to be elected.

If you count all the times Jesus referred to greed for money, you will find that he talked about it more than anything else except the Kingdom of God. And the thing he kept saying over and over was very simple: Greed destroys your soul.

Wise old Plato didn't think money was very important. When he wrote the world's first and most famous political utopia, the *Republic,* he spent only two pages talking about economics, but over forty pages talking about music and theology.

About ten years ago our babysitter asked me to speak for three minutes into her tape recorder about my heroes, for her English project. I said some obvious things about Jesus, Socrates, and my father, and she was effusively grateful. It turned out I was the only person among the twenty she had interviewed who admitted having any heroes at all! Our world is a world without heroes. We've seen Watergate, Jim and Tammy Bakker, Jimmy Swaggart, and Gary Hart. Even our few real heroes of the recent past—John F. Kennedy and Martin Luther King—turn out to have been adulterers, cheating on their wives and lying about it. Who can expect anyone to take morality seriously any more?

The answer to that question is: God. God expects you to be moral. His standards haven't changed, even if ours have.

He's not like us; he doesn't follow the fashion page. He doesn't read the *Times;* he reads the eternities. In fact, he writes them.

At the end of the nineteenth century, there was great expectation that the century to come, the twentieth, would be the best in history. The world looked forward to the abolition of war, poverty, and ignorance. Many Christians felt the same way (though they should have known better if they had read their Bibles); one liberal theological journal was founded with the title *The Christian Century.* Well, *has* it been "the Christian century"?

A more realistic picture would seem to be the one given by one of the child visionaries at Medjugorge, who said that the Devil had asked God for one century for his own, and God gave him the twentieth.

This was supposed to be the century of humanism, of respect and compassion for human life. Instead, it has been the century of genocide. Of all the atrocities of this century, that is the one that has directly affected most lives, by snuffing out the lives of over a hundred million innocent people—more than the entire population of the human race before relatively recent history—in the name of some political or racial ideology. Millions of Armenians, Jews, Chinese, Russians, and Cambodians were the victims of systematic policies of mass murder in our century. So much blood calls out to God from the ground into which it has been spilled—it is literally mind-boggling.

This was supposed to be the century to end war. Instead, it saw a new invention: the *World* War. The first two were the most devastating wars in history. And the next two? Someone has said, I don't know what weapons they'll use in World War Three, but I know what weapons they'll use in World War Four: sticks and stones.

This was supposed to be the century to abolish poverty and starvation. Instead, the gap between the rich and the poor has widened and starvation has increased. Modern technology, communications, and transportation did *not* improve the human situation. Why? Because these things carried not only healing but also hurting, for they carried, as they must, the whole human heart with all its innate diseases (the source of what Christians call Original Sin).

This was supposed to be the century to abolish ignorance through mass education. Instead, it has been the century of propaganda, mass movements, conformism, slavery to fashion, and the standardization of thinking.

This was supposed to be the Century of Man. Instead, it threatens to become the century of "the abolition of man" (to quote C.S. Lewis' prophetic title). If "God is dead," how can the image of God survive?

When you leave a room, the mirror stops reflecting your image. When God is banished from our world, the image of God, the human soul, is banished with him.

We are living in the last days, in the split second between the departure of the person from the room and the disappearance of his image in the mirror, between the death of God and the death of his image. This time cannot last for long, just as the mirror cannot continue to reflect the image of the absent person for more than a split second.

A GOOD MAN CAN LIVE IN THEM

The reader by now has almost certainly gotten exactly the opposite impression from the one I want to convey. Does this book so far sound like doomsday pessimism and despair? If so, please re-read the quotation at the beginning of this chapter: "The times are *never* so bad that a good man cannot live in them." That is my point—not simply that the times are bad, but that they are not so bad; not so bad that they make it impossible to be good. Bad times are no excuse for bad choices and bad lives.

Moral rules and ideals are not designed for good times but

for bad times. In very good times and a very good society, we don't need moral rules as much. They are like the laws of the state: you need them most not when people are good but when people are bad, to protect people against badness. Morality is the fence God put up near life's cliffs, not in safe, level places. When the road goes through flat country it needs no roadside barriers, but it needs them when it goes down mountains and into canyons.

I wonder sometimes whether God might not deliberately let the times get so bad just so that a good man can live in them. Good people, good ethics, and good moral characters are not only *for* bad times, they are also *from* bad times, they are produced by bad times, as diamonds are produced by centuries and tons of pressure, and steel is produced by high heat. I think God in his wisdom deliberately allows bad times, troubles, trials, and temptations precisely to hammer out saints on the anvil of suffering in the furnace of wickedness. He both provides good men for bad times and bad times for good men. The bad times are a "vale of soul-making" and the good souls that are made in that dark valley heal the world and bring light into the valley. The world is a giant saint-making machine, and saints are the ones who in turn change the world.

The process works both ways, for if it worked only one way, if the saints succeeded in making the world good and that's all, then life would be so joyful and goodness would be so obviously rewarded that being a saint would be so easy that it would be hard.

Think for a moment about how hard it would be to become a saint if it were easy. If there were no wall to push up against, how could you develop your muscles? If there were no sparring partner to fight against, how could you develop yourself as a fighter? If there were no suffering in the world, how could you develop compassion? If there were no difficulties, how could you develop courage? If there were no temptation (*e.g.*, to lie) how could virtue (*e.g.*, telling the truth) be precious? If sanctity didn't cost anything, how could it be worth anything? *Only* in a bad world can we become good. Bad times are for good people.

But the other half of the process is just as true: good people are for bad times. For the essence of goodness is unselfish love, self-forgetful charity. That means that sanctity is not for the sake of the saint but for the sake of the sinner, just as the health of the doctor is for the sake of the patient. The real moral reason for my being moral is not for me but for others. Good parents are good parents, for instance, only if their first concern is their children's goodness, not their own. Parents become good by being primarily concerned for their children's goodness. Good friends seek the good of each other before their own good; that's the only way they can attain their own true good. Good lovers forget themselves and even their own joy, in loving and thinking only of the beloved; and only thus can true joy come to them. The only deep and lasting pleasures in this life (and in the next!) are always self-forgetful.

So bad times are for good people and good people are for bad times. Crises are for goodness and goodness is for crises. All the saints lived in the middle of crises—if not global crises, at least personal crises. Augustine lived through both kinds and wrote his two great masterpieces to show how a good man was to live in bad times. His *Confessions,* in its own words, was written to show us "out of what depths You [God] rescue a man." *The City of God* was written to show us that even when the whole world comes tumbling down around us, even when Rome and civilization falls and tomorrow morning is the Dark Ages—even then we are to look up and work and hope and be joyful, because we are citizens not of the dying world but of the living City of God, "the city that has foundations, whose builder and maker is God," the city to which God incarnate has promised, "The gates of Hell shall not prevail against it." While we live in the dying City of the World, we must live by the principles of the imperishable City of God. We need Heaven-sent ethics for a Hell-bent world.

Times of crisis like ours are not evening times, times for going to bed, but morning times, times to rise up and grab our weapons. The battle cry has sounded. The fateful day of decision has dawned. The joy of good battle should be upon us.

Morals: principles of right & wrong.
Ethics dealing with good & evil
& with moral duty.

TWO

Decisions, Decisions, Decisions: How to Grow a Moral Backbone

NO MORALITY WITHOUT CHOICE

Morality is like a road map for living. There would be no point to a road map if we were not traveling down real physical roads. And there would be no point to morality unless we were traveling down equally real spiritual roads. Physical roads fork, and that's when you need road maps: to guide you to choose which fork to take. Moral roads also fork, and that's why you need moral road maps: for choosing which fork to take in the road of life.

Not all choices are moral choices. Most choices, in fact, are not moral choices. Shall I buy a Sony or a Zenith TV? Shall we eat chicken or hamburger tonight? Shall we set the alarm for 6 or 6:15? These are choices that are "personal" in the sense that they are relative to the person. For me the right choice may be a Zenith, since I can't afford a Sony; for you, the right choice may be a Sony. I choose chicken, you choose hamburger, and neither of us is wrong. Non-moral choices are often "personal" in this sense: relative to the individual person or the group rather than absolute; subjective rather than objective; individual rather than universal.

But moral choices are not like that, as I shall try to prove in the next chapter. Moral choices are choices between what is really, objectively right and what is really, objectively wrong. That's why we feel guilty when we make wrong moral choices, but not when we make wrong non-moral choices. We may feel *shame* when we find out that we should have bought a cheaper TV or should have taken a different physical road, a short cut; but *shame* is not *guilt.*

Of course, moral choices are "personal" in the sense that the individual person has to make them, and has responsibility for them; no one else has. But they are not "personal" in the sense that their rightness or wrongness is relative to the person who makes them. Moral choices are "personal" in the way that your answers to questions on a physics test are: they are personal in the sense that *you* take the test, and *you* are given your own individual grade. There is a right answer to each physics question; you can choose the right answer, but it is not your choosing which *makes* the answer right. The answer exists as the right answer independently of you.

Of course, making moral choices in life is also *different* from making choices on a physics test. There's no piece of paper in front of you. But there *is* a world in front of you. Morality is about the real world.

Another difference is that the right answers to questions about physics can be proved by mathematical calculation, sense observation, and laboratory experiments, but the right answer to questions about morality cannot be proved in this way. But that does not mean there *is* no right answer. The right answers to *many* questions cannot be proved this way. For example, the right answer to a question on a history test cannot be proved by mathematics, immediate sense observation, and laboratory experiments. You can't prove that Julius Caesar was a Roman emperor by arithmetic, or by seeing him alive today, or by putting him in a test tube. Yet there *is* a right answer, an objectively true answer, to the question of whether or not Julius Caesar was a Roman emperor. Moral questions also have right and wrong answers, just as questions about physics or history do; but the method of finding and proving the right answers is different in each case.

So morality implies choice, and moral choice implies a real right and wrong to choose between.

NO CHOICE WITHOUT FREE WILL

What else is implied by moral choices? Freedom of will. If we are robots, if we are machines, if we are totally programmed and pushed around by outside forces, if we are nothing but passive victims whose destinies and alternatives are determined and limited by heredity and environment, then morality makes no sense at all. You don't preach morality to machines. You don't praise or blame people for their behavior if they had no choice in the matter. The simplest proof that the human will is free to choose is this: if we are not free to choose, then all our ordinary language about morality is totally meaningless. Every sentence with words in it like *should, ought, shouldn't, right, wrong, good, evil, obligation, guilt, innocence,*—even "please"—are meaningless. You don't say "Please pass the mustard" to a machine. If you have a mustard-passing machine, you just push its button and it passes you the mustard. If people are like machines, then the only way to talk to them or treat them is by force, by pushing buttons. The consequence of denying free will and seeing people as machines to be properly programmed is totalitarian dictatorship and slavery.

That, by the way, is why philosophers and sociologists and psychologists who teach that we are not really free to make choices but are rather "determined" (caused, pushed around passively and unfreely) by our environment and our heredity, are causing more damage to the human moral conscience than a war would. The weapons we must use to fight against such a concept are not physical weapons, of course, but ideas. But fight we must, if we want to preserve our humanity against the barbarians within our own gates.

Of course, people who deny the existence of free will are not necessarily wicked people. They are often just confused and misled. But they nevertheless do tremendous damage to anyone who accepts their premise and is therefore led to believe their slavish and dictatorial conclusions.

NO FREE WILL WITHOUT SOUL

So there is no morality without choice, and no choice without free will. Further, there is no free will without a soul, or spirit, or mind. If we are only bodies; if the mind is only the brain; if we are nothing but highly evolved animals; if we are made in the image of King Kong rather than King God; then we are not free. For nothing merely material is free.

Simple matter moves by being pushed. We move by being pulled by ideals. Stones and planets move by pushes from without; living things—plants and animals—move by being pushed from within. But both move only by being pushed. Animals are pushed by their instincts, which are caused by chemicals, nerves, genes, or electrical charges in their brains. But we are moved by our mind contemplating an ideal. We are pulled by the ideal, not pushed by instinct merely. We are moved from up ahead, not just from behind.

The only part of us that has free will is the soul, not the body. So if we are only bodies, if the soul is unreal, then so is free will, and so is moral choice, and so is morality.

A materialist may be a moral person in practice, but his materialism gives him no basis for morality. He is inconsistent. If he practiced in his life what he preached in his materialistic philosophy, he would act like an animal, not like a human being.

Once again, we see that bad philosophies can be deadly enemies of humanity. If we want civilization to continue, if we want the barbarism and violence and crime to cease, we must philosophize well. We must do a lot more too, but we must do no less. For if we believe in a materialistic philosophy that teaches us to *think* of ourselves as merely clever animals, then we will sooner or later realize that there is no reason any more to *act* like anything more than a clever animal. For "ideas have consequences."

We all need a philosophy because before we can have a Christian life we must have a Christian mind. Before we can choose the good, we must know the good. Blind choice is not moral choice.

You don't need a genius IQ or a PhD to philosophize. You just need to be honest and face the questions children ask. Everyone was once a philosopher, as a child. Listen to their questions: *Why* must I be good? How do I *know* that this is good, or bad? *How* can I stop being bad? These are profoundly philosophical questions, and if children can ask them, so can you. This book is written for ordinary people who want to develop a Christian mind to provide a foundation for their moral choices and a guide to their living.

To live, you must choose. To choose, you must have a reason to choose one path rather than another. To have a reason, you must have some philosophy.

BUT MUST I CHOOSE?

Yes. Free choice is inescapable. We are "condemned to freedom," as Sartre put it.

Why the negative language ("condemned")? Because there is something in us that fears freedom. If we are free, we are responsible. We can't pass the buck to others and blame our society, or our parents, or the government. Our problem is laziness.

That's why dictatorship has always been such a popular form of government. Did you think that the only reason there have been so many dictators throughout history, and so little democracy, was because the minority of power-mad, selfish people somehow always mysteriously get the power to control and put down the vast majority of freedom-loving people? No, it is because the majority allows them, accepts them, even sometimes elects them, as Hitler was democratically elected.

Most people love freedom when it means being able to do whatever they feel like doing. But they don't love freedom when it means the responsibility of making moral choices and living with the results. Freedom is not easy. But today we want everything to be easy. That's why our political freedom is currently in great danger. Freedom is not in danger in places like Poland today, because it is not easy there. Poles know the value of freedom. They had to struggle for it, and pay for it.

But whether or not we have political freedom, everyone has moral freedom. Every human being has the free will to choose between good and evil, and the responsibility to do so. That's essential to human nature. That's why we are all "condemned to freedom."

Another way of seeing why we cannot avoid free choice is to remember that we live within time. We are constantly moving through time. When you're moving down a road and you come to a fork in the road, you must choose one fork or the other, unless you can just stop or go back. But we can't stop the flow of time, and we can't turn back into the past. Time moves us on. Our whole life on earth is a life in time, in motion. That's why we *must* choose. We have no choice about that.

This is especially true about the single most important choice you can ever make in your life. You will make three choices, sometime between your birth and your death, that will change your whole life. They are (1) the choice of a God to believe in, (2) the choice of a mate to marry, and (3) the choice of a career to work in. You can choose not to work at anything; and you can choose not to marry anyone; but you can't choose not to believe in something. If it's not the true God, it will have to be one of our society's many false gods: money, sex, drugs, power, prestige, or whatever. Something or somebody has to be your Number One.

But why can't you just avoid the question of God? An agnostic is a person who tries to do just that: avoid choosing either yes or no, either belief or unbelief, either theism or atheism. "Agnosticism" means "not knowing," and the agnostic sounds very reasonable in saying that we just don't know for sure whether God is real or not, so it's foolish to bet either for God or against God. Just don't bet at all.

Many people in our society take this position. It's much more popular than atheism. Atheism makes a definite choice. It bets against God. It lives as if there is no God. That's a choice, a commitment. It's popular in our society to avoid choice and commitment. That's why agnosticism is more popular than atheism. If you are not an agnostic yourself, you certainly know many people who are. This is how they think:

"Nobody can prove God, so believers are wrong. And nobody can disprove God either. So the right thing to do is just not to choose. It's like being the captain of a ship at sea, searching for home port—the Truth—and not knowing which of the two ports in sight is home. The captain could choose to sail into one port, but he may be wrong. The reasonable thing to do is to stay out at sea and wait until the weather clears so that he can see which port is his true home, *then* sail into it."

This sounds very reasonable. But it forgets one thing. The ship of life is moving. The sea is time, and it is not still. The ship is drifting with the current. You can't stay still by not choosing. If you don't choose, the current will choose for you.

Furthermore, your fuel will run out soon. There is a point of no return somewhere up ahead on the current you're drifting down. That point is where all your fuel is gone. It's called death. At that point, agnosticism is impossible. It's too late. At that point agnosticism becomes atheism.

God is unknowable

The point is that because you live in the unstoppable flow of time which moves only forward, you have only two choices, not three. You can choose to believe, or not to believe. To "choose" *not* to choose eventually results in choosing no. Suppose God is like Romeo and you are like Juliet. God proposes marriage to your soul. Now suppose Juliet responds to every marriage proposal from Romeo by saying, "I choose not to choose today. I say to you neither yes nor no. Try me tomorrow." After seventy years of tomorrows, they both will die, *un*married. Juliet has really said no. Not saying yes to a marriage proposal means eventually saying no, because there are only so many tomorrows.

If we lived forever in time, on earth, without death, we could postpone choices forever. Would that be wonderful? No, that would be terrible. If we postponed choices, we would never learn to choose, and never become truly human. For without free choice we are not fully human. Therefore, if the scientists ever discovered how to make us immortal by artificial means, they would destroy our humanity.

So we *must* choose, either to believe or not to believe. The third option is a fake. Not to choose is to choose to say no.

The same is true of every moral choice. There seem to be three options: (1) to choose good, (2) to choose evil, and (3) not to choose. That is, to be (1) moral, (2) immoral, or (3) amoral, nonmoral. But (3) is often really the same as (2), when it is due not to ignorance but to a refusal. Sins of omission are just as bad as sins of commission. Standing on the sidelines while a great battle between good and evil is going on, as it is right now in our society—that indifference is truly evil.

But most people don't see this. When they hear the word "evil" they think only of some monster like Hitler. They don't think amorality is evil, only immorality. If they are amoral, they think of themselves as good people, as long as they're not *im*moral. Even if they're indifferent to morality, even if they hardly ever think about good and evil, even if they have chosen not to choose between good and evil, they don't think of this as evil. Their morality is: As long as you don't hurt other people, you're a good person. In other words, if you act like a turtle, you can still be a good person. What nonsense! But what popular nonsense!

Most of the people we know in our society are not immoral but amoral. How many people do you know who deliberately choose evil rather than good, as the habitual pattern of their lives? Probably few or none. I know there is an alarming and increasing number of drug dealers, wife-beaters, child-molesters, pimps, and rapists. But most of the people most of us know are "nice" people. Indeed, that adjective is almost always the one we use: "Oh, he's a nice person. . . ." But being a *nice* person is not necessarily the same as being a *good* person, a moral person. To be nice means only to be socially acceptable. The opposite of "nice" is "nasty." But being good means much more than just not being nasty.

How do most of us decide what to do and what not to do, what to say and what not to say, most of the time? By three standards: (1) social fads and fashions, others' expectations, peer pressure, "everybody's doing it"; (2) our feelings ("it can't be wrong if it feels so right"); and (3) our desire for the easiest, most pleasant, least troublesome life. I think most of us use these three standards far more often than the standard of good and evil, right and wrong, in deciding what to do. If we're asked why we did something, how often do we answer, "Because it was *right*"?

Even our popular guides and teachers won't use words

like "right" and "wrong." They use sociological gobble-degook and psychobabble like "appropriate behavior" or "acceptable behavior" instead of plain moral common sense.

Instead of teaching morality to our children, we need to be taught morality by them sometimes, since they still have the innate moral instincts we've thrown away. I remember once driving a station wagon full of morally wise pre-schoolers and a morally bankrupt teacher to a museum. The teacher was a bright, nice, modern girl with all the right psychological moves, but she couldn't control one kid who was terrorizing all the others. She kept telling the little bully that her behavior was "inappropriate." Finally, one of the other kids said to the teacher, loudly, "Why don't you tell her?" "Tell her what?" asked the teacher. "Don't tell her she's 'in-propriate.' Tell her she's *wrong!*" I felt like clapping.

Not wearing a suit jacket to a fancy restaurant is inappropriate. Skipping out without paying the check is wrong. It's incredible, but the more educated you are in our society, the more likely it is that your mind will confuse these two things that even a child knows are different.

One who never uses the words "right" and "wrong" is a moral wimp, not a good person. Good people are not made from wimps; good people are made from bad people. Saints are made from sinners. Being a sinner is closer to being a saint than being a wimp is.

Matthew was a "publican"—*i.e.,* a tax collector who was probably a thief. The apostle Paul was a persecutor of Christians. Mary Magdalene was demon possessed. Augustine was a playboy. Francis of Assisi was a fop. Ignatius of Loyola was a hired killer (*i.e.,* a mercenary soldier).

Those who choose evil can change, and choose good—just as a car moving left can change, and move right. But those who don't choose either good or evil are like a car that's stopped. It's much easier to get a car that's moving left to move right than to get a car that's stopped to move right.

Not making moral choices means not moving at all, not

developing any moral muscle at all. Making wrong moral choices means moving wrongly, developing your moral muscles wrongly, but at least developing them. Morality is like playing for the home team, the good guys, and immorality is like playing for the enemy, the other team; but amorality is like not playing the game at all. Immorality has a bad conscience, but at least it has a conscience. Amorality has no working or waking conscience at all. That's why it's even farther away from morality than immorality is.

A white water raft has to actively cooperate with the river in moving downstream. A leaf that fell into the water is simply passive, drifting. A salmon swimming upstream is as active as the raft, but in the opposite direction. The stream is like Goodness. The raft is like morality, the leaf is like amorality, and the salmon is like immorality. At least the salmon has muscles, and life, and passion.

The state of soul that is farthest from great sanctity is not great sin but great sluggishness. Moral lethargy is more disgusting to God than wickedness. God said that, not me. Read Revelation 3:15-16.

Righteous indignation is dangerous, because it easily turns into *un*righteous indignation. But someone who is *incapable* of righteous indignation is incapable of righteousness. It is not "compassionate" to have no indignation toward the drug dealer who sold crack to the teenager who just died of an overdose, or to the lawyer who got him freed. Compassion for the victim equals indignation at the crime.

WHY ARE WE SUCH MORAL WIMPS?

Because we've misunderstood compassion.

Compassion is supposed to be a maximum, but we've turned it into a minimum. Compassion is supposed to be more than justice; we've made it into something less than justice.

What is the work of compassion? Mercy and forgiveness.

Mercy presupposes justice. Mercy tempers justice, it does not replace it. Forgiveness also presupposes justice. Forgiveness has to have something to forgive, some real wrong. If sin and evil and real wrong are superstitions, then forgiveness is impossible.

We are supposed to have compassion and mercy and forgiveness toward sinners, as God does. But we are not supposed to use "compassion" as an excuse to deny the existence of sin. God never does that. But the modern world does.

Every time someone makes a moral judgment, they are criticized for lacking "compassion," and labeled with one or more of modern man's three F-words: fascist, fanatic, and fundamentalist (the latter must be pronounced with a sneer).

There is a strong double standard in most of our society, especially the media. If anyone dares to suggest that homosexual intercourse is wrong, that person is a homophobic fanatic. But if the same person were to denounce political corruption, or industrial espionage, or sudden tax hikes, he would be considered enlightened and responsible. If someone in Operation Rescue puts his body on the line and goes to jail to save live, human, unborn babies from being murdered in an abortion clinic, he, or even she, is said to lack compassion and sensitivity for women. But if someone condemns apartheid, that person is not called uncompassionate to white racists. If people condemn divorce, as Jesus did, they are thought to be condemning divorcees. But if they condemn the destruction of Brazilian rain forests, they are not thought to be condemning Brazilians.

If anyone dares to call promiscuity "promiscuity" instead of a "sexually active lifestyle," they are immediately labeled narrow-minded and uncompassionate. If anyone suggests that AIDS should be treated as other communicable diseases are treated—*e.g.*, reported to insurance companies, or sometimes quarantined—they are accused of trying to revive the Spanish Inquisition. What's going on here?

Apparently the substitution of compassion for morality applies only to one area: sex. We do not tolerate inside trading by stock brokers, but we do tolerate sodomy by congressmen (at least in Massachusetts). We do not tolerate an unbalanced budget, but we tolerate broken marriages. We do not tolerate theft, but we tolerate adultery. What's going on here, as we shall explore more deeply in Chapter Nine, is that our society is very serious about money and very loose about sex. Money is holy but sex is secular, money is worthy of respect but sex is a mere medium of exchange. In other words, it treats money like sex and sex like money.

Doctors are not called uncompassionate if they give their patients a diagnosis of cancer or a prescription for an operation. Yet doctors of the soul are called uncompassionate if they give a diagnosis of sin and prescription of repentance. Yet the two cases are exactly parallel. The only difference is that sin is the cancer of the soul, not of the body. Our society no longer believes in or cares about the soul.

Would you want your doctor to be as compassionate to the disease as he is to the patient? Would you want him or her to be compassionate to your cancer cells? Of course not. But we want our moral teachers to be "compassionate" rather than "judgmental" about the spiritual cancers, the sins and evils, that we are addicted to, especially the two that dominate modern life, lust and greed.

We must "love the sinner and hate the sin." This is not a hairsplitting, abstract, technical distinction for scholars and theologians. It is crucial and practical. If we love the sin, we do *not* love the sinner, just as if we love the cancer, we do not love the patient.

There is a proper kind of hate. Even God has "wrath" (unless Scripture lies). God does not hate any *sinner*, not even the worst. Jesus loved Judas to the last, and called him "friend." God loves Stalin and Hitler and Charles Manson, as David loved his rebel son Absalom, and for the same reason: He is our Father. But God hates *sin*, and so should we. To hate *people* is to lack compassion. To hate *nothing*, not even sin, is to be nothing, to be a wimp.

We must relearn how to hate. We are too tolerant: not of humans but of dehumanization, of injustice and oppression and greed and lust and all other forms of selfishness, however popular among certain groups. We must learn to love human selves much more and to love human selfishness much less. We must learn to discriminate, to hate not the self but the selfishness, not the sinner but the sin.

Choosing is hard for us moderns because it means discriminating, refusing, saying no to one path as we say yes to the other. We cannot meditate too often on Psalm 1, the psalm about the two ways to live. It is life's first and most basic lesson, and our society has unlearned it because we substitute a vague, undiscriminating "compassion" for a clear and discriminating love.

> Blessed is the man
>> who walks not in the counsel of the wicked,
> nor stands in the way of sinners,
>> nor sits in the seat of scoffers;
> but his delight is in the law of the LORD
>> and on his law he meditates day and night.
> He is like a tree
>> planted by streams of water,
> that yields its fruit in its season,
>> and its leaf does not wither.
> In all that he does, he prospers.
>
> The wicked are not so,
>> but are like chaff which the wind
>> drives away.
> Therefore the wicked will not

stand in the judgment,
nor sinners in the congregation of the righteous;
for the LORD watches over the way of
the righteous,
but the way of the wicked will perish. (Psalm 1)

Dostoyevski says, "Love in action is a harsh and dreadful thing compared with love in dreams." For love in action has to choose, while love in dreams can just dream vague, comfortable, all-embracing dreams.

To love every ideal equally is to be indifferent to truth. To approve every lifestyle equally is to be indifferent to how to live. To love animals equally with people is to be indifferent to people. (Some people even love animals *more* than people, when they want to save the whales but abort the babies. "Be a hero; save a whale. Save a baby; go to jail.")

It's simply not true that "all you need is love." You also need truth. A surgeon needs more than love. He also needs light. That's what this book is about.

Part Two

Principles:
The Fundamental Issue,
Moral Absolutes

THREE

Are There Any Moral Absolutes?: Finding Black and White in a World of Grays

THIS IS NOT AN ABSTRACT, THEORETICAL QUESTION for professors to argue. It is the most concrete, practical question for our civilization. For no civilization has ever survived without moral absolutes.

To disbelieve in all moral absolutes is implicitly to be a snob, to call all cultures fools, and to call that vision folly which has guided the lives of nearly everyone who has ever lived on this planet.

We are snobs if we call people who have been educated by life, tradition, experience, and family "backward" or "primitive." William F. Buckley said, "If I had to choose between being ruled by the first five hundred names in the Harvard faculty directory or the first five hundred names in the Boston Public Telephone Directory, I would unhesitatingly choose the latter."

Buckley's choice is a democratic one, for it prefers the judgments of the majority. It is also democratic because it prefers more traditional opinions, and tradition is simply "the democracy of the dead" (as Chesterton put it), giving the dead a vote too.

MORAL *LAWS* OR MORAL *VALUES*?

We can see that we have abandoned belief in moral absolutes by looking at one key change in our language about morality: we no longer talk about moral *laws*, but about moral *values*. This may seem unimportant, but it is momentous. For *laws* are objectively real; they come from above us and command us. The formula for a moral law is "Thou shalt" or "Thou shalt not." But *values* have no such strong bite, no absolute demand. They suggest something subjective, not objective: "my" values or "your" values or "society's" values. Values come *from* us; laws come *to* us. We *invent* values, but we are *under* laws. Values are nice ideals to aspire to if we wish; laws tell us what we ought to do whether we like it or not.

We no longer like to talk about moral laws, values, and about moral absolutes. But we do like to talk about morality, a morality without absolutes. But a morality without absolutes is not a morality at all. "Do as you please" is not morality, "do what you ought" is morality. "Do whatever you think will have the best consequences" is not morality; it is calculation. "Do what works" is not morality, it is efficiency. Morality *means* something different from doing what we please, or what we calculate will turn out all right, or what works; morality means doing what we ought to do. Morality is not optional, like a "value," but obligatory, like a law. A morality without laws and obligations is simply a confusion, like a triangle without angles.

Why then do people say there are no absolutes? Why do they say morality is a matter of grays, not blacks and whites?

Why do they say that making moral choices is so terribly complex and uncertain and difficult? The answer is simple: as Chesterton said, making moral decisions is always a terribly confusing thing—to someone without principles.

This book is not about complex moral dilemmas. There are really only a few really complex moral dilemmas for most of us. Ninety-nine out of a hundred of our moral choices are quite simple and clear, if only we stop rationalizing. This book is practical, not theoretical; therefore it addresses the moral choices we actually make, the ordinary, humdrum choices like whether or not to cheat on your wife or your income tax, not those fascinating academic exercises so cherished by "Values Clarification" like whom do you throw out of the lifeboat when the food runs out, or how to prevent nuclear war. Academic exercises have no bite of guilt in them; ordinary moral choices do. No one is ever *wrong* in Values Clarification. But in real life, everyone has some guilt, some moral wrongness, and some sin. For in real life there are moral laws, but in academic exercises there are only moral "values."

THREE PARTS TO MORALITY

Suppose Hitler sincerely believed he was doing the world a great good by exterminating the Jews: why doesn't that make it right?

Suppose a billionaire gives millions to shelter the homeless, but only to avoid having to pay it in income tax; is that a morally good deed or not?

Suppose a loving husband makes love to his wife, but at a time the doctor warns him is medically dangerous. Is this a good deed or a bad deed?

Thomas Aquinas has a good answer to these questions. He says that there are three parts to morality, and all three

parts must be good for any act to be morally good. The three are (1) the objective act itself, (2) the subjective motive, and (3) the situation, or circumstances.

Moral laws can help you with the first part. They define which kinds of acts are good or bad, not because of your motive or intention, but because of the act itself.

The second factor in determining morality is the intention, or motive. The first factor, the nature of the act itself, is objective; the second factor, the intention, is subjective. So when people say morality is subjective, they're partly right. But when they say it's *all* subjective, they're simply wrong. And both the objective and the subjective factors are moral absolutes. We must *always* have good intentions, just as we must always do good things. Hate, greed, lust, envy, sloth, wrath, pride, or despair are absolutely wrong motives, just as murder, theft, etc. are absolutely wrong deeds.

But in addition to these two absolute factors, there is a third factor, which is relative: the situation, or circumstances. These are endlessly changing, and we have to make up our own mind how best to apply the moral absolutes to relative situations. For instance, in one situation, charity to the poor may mean giving a tramp money for food, but in another situation it may mean refusing him money because he'd use it on alcohol. Or charity to the poor may mean contributing to a large charitable organization, or electing a certain political candidate.

This is the factor that is indeed uncertain. For instance, what helps the poor more, Democratic economics of more direct anti-poverty programs, or Republican economics of feeding the economy as a whole? The answer is not certain, as it is certain what acts and what motives are good and bad.

All three factors must be morally right for the act to be right. If you do the wrong thing, it is wrong, even if your motive is sincere. Perhaps Hitler was sincere in his desire to "improve" the world; perhaps Charles Manson or Jim Jones sincerely thought they were doing God's work. But what they did was wrong. You can be sincere and dead wrong. You can be sincere and insane.

If you do the right thing for the wrong reason, it is also wrong, just as wrong as doing the wrong thing for the right reason Giving money away only to avoid paying taxes, for instance, is doing a morally good thing but not for a morally good reason.

Finally, the circumstances must also be right. Making love to your spouse out of love but when it is medically dangerous is wrong. If any one of these three factors is wrong, the act is wrong; if all three are right, the act is right.

Three popular systems of ethics today emphasize just one of these three factors and ignores the other two. Unthinking *legalism* concentrates on only the first factor, the objective moral law, ignoring the subjective motive and the relative circumstances. Moral *subjectivism* concentrates on only the second factor, the subjective motive, and ignores the other two. (This is probably the most popular morality today: "if only your motive is sincere and loving, nothing else matters.") Finally, *situation ethics* says the situation (or the situation plus the motive) determines everything. This denies factor one, the objective nature of the act itself.

THREE QUESTIONS:
ABSOLUTE? OBJECTIVE? UNIVERSAL?

We have been thinking about three related issues, and we should distinguish them: (1) are there any moral *absolutes*? (2) is morality *objective*? and (3) is morality *universal*?

The opposite of *absolute* is *relative*. "Thou shalt not murder" is an absolute. It is true and valid in itself, not relative to anything else, not if and only if you feel like it, or somebody told you, or the weather is nice. The justice of a war, on the other hand, is relative—to whether it is aggressive or defensive, unnecessary or necessary, destructive of innocents or not, and whether more injustice is done than is corrected. (I am here assuming the common-sensical tradition of the "just war theory." Both militarists and pacifists would disagree with it.)

"Honor your father and mother" is a moral absolute. But "support your father and mother" is relative—to their need and your ability.

"Thou shalt not commit adultery" is a moral absolute. It does not depend on your feelings or social mores or consequences. It does not suddenly become right when you feel in love, or when society tolerates it, or if it would make you a million dollars. But "spouses should share their lives together" is relative to their social customs and cultural content.

The opposite of our second term, "objective," is "subjective." Something that's objective is independent of us, our knowledge, our feelings, and our choices. "Trees are green" and "2+3=5" and "Kennedy was shot in 1963" are objective truths. My headache, my feelings for the Boston Red Sox (these two examples are pretty much identical), my opinions about the future, and my liking basset hounds and disliking poodles are subjective: states of consciousness, in me, dependent on me, neither true nor false in themselves.

Moral *intentions* are subjective because *all* intentions are subjective. But the moral law tells me that some intentions are absolutely right (*e.g.,* love and justice) and others absolutely wrong (*e.g.,* hating persons and selfishness).

Moral *laws* are not subjective, but objective. Moral *motives* or intentions are subjective.

The opposite of the third term, "universal," is "particular." "Universal" means always, in all situations, with no exceptions and no change. "Particular" means only in some situations or times, changeable. Situations are particular, laws are universal. You should *never* steal, but in some situations the government should increase taxes and in some situations it should not. Some taxing is stealing, some is not.

Moral laws are absolute, objective, and universal. That is the proposition denied by the modern world. The modern world wants to believe that moral laws are relative, subjective, and particular. That way, we are not under an absolute obligation to obey them. They depend on our subjective belief or unbelief in them, and I can always make particular exceptions when supposedly universal rules would limit my "freedom" too much for my liking.

WHY DO PEOPLE DISBELIEVE IN MORAL ABSOLUTES?

If "why" means "what motives impel them?" the answer is most often *convenience,* I think. All of us know from our own experience that hard, unyielding moral absolutes are often very inconvenient. We would very much like to bend the laws a bit; therefore we bend our *beliefs* about the law. It takes only a little knowledge of modern psychology to reveal how much we all rationalize rather than reason, how often our arguments are supports for our desires rather than honest searches after truth.

A second motive is peer pressure and conformity to fashion. If your college philosophy professor disbelieves in moral absolutes and your parents believe in them (which is the usual situation), you probably want to be "up-to-date" and sophisticated and go with the new-found "wisdom" of your professor.

But these are not good *reasons,* only *motives.* They are not objective logical arguments but subjective pyschological causes. What *arguments* do some people (like college philosophy professors) use to try to prove there are no moral absolutes, and how can they be refuted?

The seven most popular arguments are the following:

1. Values are relative to cultures. Different cultures have different values. It is provincial to deny this.

2. Values come from society, by a process now called "conditioning." (It used to be called "education," but

"education" is done to free human beings, while "conditioning" is done to rats.)

3. If you want to be free, you must "create your own values." If values are "imposed on you," you are not free.

4. Absolutists and absolutism are intolerant, hard, and uncompassionate. Relativism and relativists are humane and tolerant.

5. Morality is a matter of individual conscience and subjective motive, not of some impersonal objective law of do's and don'ts that is the same for everyone.

6. What's right and wrong varies depending on the situation.

7. Scientific thinking discovers no moral absolutes. They do not appear to the senses, and denying them does not violate any law of logic.

Now here are the refutations of these arguments.

1. Different cultures have different *opinions* about what is right and wrong. Nazi Germany thought genocide right. Cannibals think eating humans is right. Americans think fornication is all right. But they're wrong about what's right! Thinking something is so doesn't make it so. *Opinions* are relative to cultures, but *truth* isn't.

In the second place, even opinions about values are not wholly relative to cultures. No culture thinks courage is bad and cowardice good, honesty bad and dishonesty good, theft and adultery and murder good. Every society has some version of the Ten Commandments. If a sociologist tells you otherwise, ask him which society has had this totally different set of values. It is true that different societies *apply* these basic values differently. For instance, in some societies suicide is thought to be courageous, in others it is thought to be cowardly. But no society prefers cowardice to courage. Some societies let a man have four wives, others only one, but no society says a man may simply take any woman he wants.

2. Does society "condition" values in us? No more than society "conditions" the multiplication table in us. Society "conditions" in us its value *opinions,* but society does not condition real values themselves.

Just because we learn something from our society does not mean that thing is socially relative. Some things are (like styles of clothing), some are not (like the rules of good health, and moral health).

3. Does freedom mean "creating your own values"? No more than it means creating your own mathematics, or your own history. *Mores* (customs) are created; *morals* (morality) are discovered. We create rules like "drive on the right," and could just as well create other rules, like "drive on the left." But we did not invent the rules of morality, any more than we invented the rules of bodily health, and we cannot change them. We cannot "creatively" make murder and lying and greed and lust good. We are *not* free to "create" values. We are free to choose to obey or disobey them. Similarly, we do not invent the rules of math, or health, but we are free to obey them or disobey them, to say 2+2=4 or 2+2=5, to eat bread or to eat dirt.

4. Absolutes *are* hard and unyielding, because they are facts. But absolutists need not be hard and unyielding (though many are). Tolerance is good, indeed; but to admit this is to admit a real, objective value: tolerance!

Relativism is *not* humane. It is tolerant *only* as long as it feels like being tolerant. Once it feels otherwise, no moral law prevents it from becoming dictatorial. If the only morality is what society dictates, then there is no moral appeal against Nazi genocide or South African racism, if the society approves these things.

5. Is morality a matter of individual conscience? Yes indeed. It is *also* a matter of objective fact: the truth of the moral law. Neither one of these two factors substitutes for the other. The law cannot make my decision for me, and I cannot make the moral law by my decisions. Remember, there are three factors in morality, not just one. One of these three factors, the moral law that tells us which acts are good and which are evil, is indeed the same for everyone and not different for different individuals. We are all judged by the same law. Morality is an equal opportunity employer.

6. What about changing situations? Just as conscience does not exclude moral law, so changing situations do not exclude moral law. In fact, situational morality presupposes a moral law. The only way to make moral sense of a situation is to apply a moral law to it. Otherwise, it is not a *situation* but a meaningless chaos.

7. Finally, it is true that scientific thinking does not discover morality. So what? Neither does poetic thinking, or musical thinking, or awareness of pain and pleasure. There are many ways of thinking, many modes of consciousness. The one that discovers morality is called conscience.

By what right does the objector assume that *only* the scientific method can prove objective truth? *That* "fact" cannot be proved by the scientific method!

What do you say to someone who is sincerely puzzled as to how we are supposed to know moral absolutes, since they do not appear to the senses? Tell him that he has inner senses too. Every normal human being discovers right and wrong by the inner eye of conscience. If someone cannot understand even that, what hope is there that he will understand anything else about morality? If a man is color blind, do we expect him to be an artist? Do we trust the tone-deaf to write our music? Then why do we listen to morally tone-deaf philosophers when they teach us that morality is merely relative and subjective? A child and a peasant know that right and wrong are not matters of taste or fashion. Only a scholar could miss such an obvious point, and only a gullible student, more eager to follow fashion than truth, could take the scholar seriously.

THE RELATIVIST'S SELF-CONTRADICTION

The relativist lets the cat out of the bag when you practice what he preaches, when you *act* toward *him* as if his own philosophy of relativism were true. He may *preach* relativism, but he expects *you to practice* absolutism. For instance, an ethics class of mine told me they thought morality was relative, and what right did I have to "impose my values" of absolutism on them? I replied, "All right. Let's run the class by your values, not mine. There are no absolutes. Moral values are subjective and relative. And my particular set of subjective personal moral values includes this one: all women in my class flunk." They immediately protested in shock: "That's unfair!" "Yes, it is unfair," I agreed. "But what do you mean by 'fair'? If fairness, or justice, is only MY value or YOUR value, then it has no universal authority over both of us. I have no right to impose MY values on you, and you have no right to impose yours on me. But if there is a universal, objective, absolute value called justice, or fairness, then it holds for both of us, and it judges me as wrong when I say all women flunk. And you can appeal to that justice in judging my rule as unfair. But if there is no such thing as absolute objective justice, then all you can mean when you protest my rule is that you don't like it, that your subjective values are different than mine. But that's not what you said. You didn't say merely that you didn't like my rule, but that it was unfair. So you do believe in moral absolutes after all, when it comes down to practice. Why do you believe that silly theory, then? Why are you hypocrites? Why don't you practice what you preach, and stop appealing to justice, or else preach what you practice, and stop denying it?"

Actually, at least one famous moral relativist was consistent even about that. Jean-Paul Sartre, the famous French atheist, protested against the Nuremberg trials of Nazi war criminals on charges of "crimes against humanity," because they were judged not by German law or French law but natural law, universal law. The trial assumed that such a universal moral law really existed. Sartre had always taught that it didn't. So he was consistent. The democracies had no right to judge the Nazis if all values were relative to different cultures or different individuals.

That was consistent. It was also moral bankruptcy—intolerable, unendurable, unlivable. Thank God for consistent moral relativists like Sartre: they show us what relativism really comes to.

FOUR

The Foundation for Moral Absolutes: Can You Be Moral without God?

W E HAVE SEEN IN THE LAST CHAPTER that it is impossible to have a real morality without moral absolutes. Is it also impossible to have moral absolutes without God? Is religion the only basis for morality?

Here is a strong argument for answering that question in the affirmative. It is the story of Ivan Karamazov, one of *The Brothers Karamazov* in that great, great novel of Dostoyevski's. Ivan's father, Fyodor Karamazov, is a thoroughly despicable character: dishonest, greedy, lustful, selfish, and violent. All four of his sons hate him. In doing so, they really hate "the Karamazov nature" in themselves, for we have all inherited that nature from our parents. (The equivalent in the Bible is what theologians call Original Sin, inherited from our forefather Adam.)

Ivan hates his father and wants him dead. He does not actually commit the murder, however, but he is responsible for it because he justifies it with his philosophy. That philosophy is atheism, which is mentally killing God the Father—a kind of substitute for killing Fyodor his earthly father.

Ivan is a brilliant mind, a philosopher. He sees the logical consequences of atheism, and teaches this philosophy: *"If there is no God, then everything is permissible."* He hopes his brother Dmitri will use this philosophy as an excuse to kill Fyodor, thus saving Ivan the dirty work.

But even though Ivan does not commit the actual murder, he is the one most responsible, just as Judas was the one most responsible for Jesus' death, not the soldiers who nailed him to the cross. It was Ivan's philosophy that took away moral law and moral restraint.

It is a dramatic, even spectacular and bloody argument for God as the only possible basis for morality. For if there is no God, each of us is his or her own God. If God is the source and basis for morality, then to take away the source and cause is to take away the effect; to take away the basis and foundation is to collapse the building.

Dostoyevski, the author, is not an atheist, but a Christian. But he agrees with this philosophy of Ivan's: IF there is no God, there is no morality. Alyosha, Ivan's good brother, who believes in God and morality, also believes that IF there were no God, there would be no morality. That's one of the reasons Alyosha believes in God. (Philosophers often use this argument for God; it is called the "Moral Argument.")

Like the famous "First Cause" argument, which reasons from God's created effects in nature back to God as the creating cause of these effects, this Moral Argument also reasons from the effect back to the cause. But this time the effect is a real and absolute morality known by conscience. The only possible cause, or source, or foundation for an absolutely binding moral law must be an absolute, divine will.

The argument seems very strong if you only admit the premise: that there is an absolute moral law, that we are under absolute moral obligation, at least to our conscience. You can get almost anyone to admit this premise: that there is at least this one moral absolute: you should never, never disobey your conscience. Conscience is an absolute. People who no longer believe the Ten Commandments are absolutes usually still believe in at least this one moral absolute: conscience.

But if you admit that, you must admit a God. For where could this absolute authority of conscience come from? Neither my own feelings nor the rules invented by my society have an absolute authority. Everyone admits that we should sometimes disobey our feelings (*e.g.*, if I feel like murdering you), and that we should sometimes disobey the rules of our society (*e.g.*, if we were in Nazi Germany). There is only one possible source of the absolute authority of conscience: it must be the voice of God.

It makes sense. If there is no divine lawgiver, there is no divine law. If there is no absolute moral cause (God), there could be no absolute moral effect (the absolute authority of conscience). If you take away the cause, you take away the effect.

So it certainly seems that religion is the only possible basis for morality.

We can state this in two different ways. We can say that the real God is the only possible basis, or cause, of real moral law; or we can say that religion, or *belief* in God, is the only possible basis for morality, or *belief* in moral law. This may seem like a hairsplitting and technical distinction, but as we shall see, it is one that is necessary to solve a serious problem.

If civilization without morality is impossible, and if morality without religion is impossible, then civilization without religion is impossible. This shows how crucial the issue is: it means that the civilization we are now living in—a secular rather than a religious civilization—is doomed.

For if our argument is correct, civilization is like a flower, morality is like a stem, and religion is like a root. The flower grows only from the stem and the stem grows only from the root. If the root dies, the stem dies, and if the stem dies, the flower dies. As ours seems to be doing.

But *is* religion the only possible basis for morality?

ARGUMENTS FOR THE "NO" ANSWER

There are three strong arguments for answering no: scriptural, observational, and philosophical. The authority of Scripture, observation of different people and cultures, and philosophical reasoning all seem to say that there can be and often is morality without religion.

First, scriptural. St. Paul says very clearly in Romans 1 that pagans, who have no divine revelation of the true God, know the moral law by reason and conscience. That's why they too are responsible before that moral law, just as Jews and Christians are.

Here are St. Paul's words:

> For God shows no partiality. All who have sinned without the law [*i.e.,* without knowledge of the Mosaic, Jewish law] will also perish without the law, and all who have sinned under the law will be judged by the law. For it is not the hearers of the law who are righteous before God, but the doers of the law who will be justified. When Gentiles who have not the law do by nature what the law requires, they are a law to themselves, even though they do not have the law. They show that what the law requires is written on their hearts, while their conscience also bears witness and their conflicting thoughts accuse or perhaps excuse them. . . . (Romans 2:11-15)

In the Old Testament too, prophets like Amos held Gentile nations responsible for what the Nuremberg trials called "crimes against humanity" (*e.g.*, rape, pillage, torture, oppression, and theft), while he held Jews responsible also for crimes against their own more specific, divinely revealed law (see Amos 1-3).

God is just. He does not judge us by what we do not know. But he does judge us by what we do know. And everyone, Jew and Gentile alike, Christian and non-Christian alike, theist and atheist alike, knows the moral law in his or her conscience. If even the nonreligious know the moral law and are morally responsible, then religion is not the only possible basis for morality.

A second reason for this conclusion is the simple observation that pagans, who have wrong and confused notions of God, and modern atheists, who do not believe in any God at all, do in fact know, often profess, and even sometimes practice a very true and high morality. Socrates is a good pagan example. He was basically an agnostic, one who claimed to know nothing about the gods. If he had only been able honestly to confess that he believed in any of the gods recognized by his society, he would not have been executed for atheism, as he was. But he could not honestly confess that he believed in Zeus, or Athena, or any god except some vague, unknowable, undefined being he called simply "*the* god." Yet Socrates both preached and practiced a morality that can only be called saintly. And he did not base it on religion.

In our own times, it is not at all evident that believers in God have a higher morality than atheists. More violent crimes, proportionately, are committed by theists than by atheists. We all know examples of hypocrisy and public scandal among religious believers. Certainly, there are many saintly believers and many notoriously immoral atheists. Even *one* saintly atheist would refute the idea that religion is the *only* possible basis for morality.

Third, the philosophical point we made in the last chapter, about everyone knowing innately and instinctively, by moral common sense, that there are moral absolutes—the point about only university professors and their students forgetting this common sense moral knowledge—seems to prove that everyone innately knows morality, whether or not they base it on religion. Ask anyone this question: If twenty sadists agree to torture one normal person, do the numbers make it right? If society says it's OK, does that make it right? Obviously not, and *everyone knows that*, deep down, until they start reading some modern philosophers. No matter what our heads may say, no matter what our philosophers may say, in our hearts we know some things are just plain wrong in themselves; that torture, *e.g.*, is wrong, not because society says so but because of what torture *is*. We know that unselfish love is right not because everyone does it (they *don't*) or "everyone says so" (they don't even do that), but because of what it is.

We all know true morality. We do not all know true religion. There is only one essential morality in the world, but many religions. Moralities differ only on secondary matters; religions differ on primary matters (like whether God has a will, and whether there is life after death). True morality is innate, but true religion is revealed.

THE SOLUTION

We have given strong arguments for both the yes and no answers to our question: Is religion the only possible basis for morality? How do we resolve the issue?

By distinguishing between the objective fact and our knowledge of it. There cannot really *be* moral absolutes without God; there cannot *be* an absolute moral law without an absolute moral lawgiver. But we can *know* the effect without knowing the cause: we can know the moral law without knowing the moral lawgiver, just as we can know God's natural effects by science without knowing God as the Creator-cause of these effects. There can't *be* the effect without the cause, but you can *know* the effect without knowing the cause.

So both sides are right. Dostoyevski is right about the objective facts. If God did not exist, a real moral law would not exist either, and everything would be permissible. But Paul is also right about our knowledge: everyone knows the moral law clearly and adequately (that's why everyone is morally responsible before the moral law), but not everyone knows the divine Lawgiver. It is one of the tasks of the Christian apologist or missionary to bring people from their knowledge of morality to a knowledge of God, as Paul did in Romans, or as C.S. Lewis did in the first part of *Mere Christianity*.

God made the moral rules, but not in an arbitrary way. He inscribed them in human nature and human knowledge. He made the rules of morality as the laws of human nature, just as he made the laws of physical nature. The law of gravity is inherent in the nature of matter. The laws of morality are inherent in the nature of man. The law of gravity is true because that's the *nature* of matter. The law of love is true because that's the *nature* of man: man was *designed* to love, as matter was designed to attract. The difference between moral laws and physical laws is that man can disobey the laws of his nature, but matter can't. Man alone has free will and moral choice.

One practical application of our solution is that Christians need not and often should not appeal to religious faith as the reason for criticizing public sins like abortion, pornography, or indifference to the poor. These are sins against God, it is true, but they are also sins against man, against human nature and natural law, and that is why we can call on all people of good will, of any religious faith or of none, to cooperate in enforcing justice, in protecting the innocent victims of crimes that kill human bodies or harm human souls. Until Christians are clear about that, they will never win in the public arena, for non-Christians will continue to think and fear, as they do now, that Christians are trying to "impose their own religious values" on others. No. Outlawing abortion or pornography no more depends on religion than outlawing assassination or cocaine.

THE PRACTICAL PROBLEM

What we've been thinking about is the theoretical problem. But there is also a practical problem. The theoretical problem is: Can there be morality without religion? And: Can you know morality without knowing religion? The practical problem is: Can you *live* morality without living religion? Can you *practice* morality without practicing religion?

Again, we seem to have a dilemma. Both answers have strong arguments to support them.

First of all, the "no" answer. Apparently, you can't practice morality apart from religion because the moral life and the religious life are essentially the same life. Objectively, they are the very life of God, divine life in the soul, our participation in God's own activity. Subjectively, they are also identical: uniting our will with God's, willing what God wills, *i.e.*, goodness. Conforming our will and life to God's is the essence of Christian morality *and* of Christian religion. The very word "religion" means binding, yoking, or relating (us and our life and our will to God's).

But the opposite answer also contains an important truth: religion cannot be identified with morality. That is basically what liberal or modernist theology does. Morality may be an indispensable part or beginning to religion, but it is not the whole or the end. As C.S. Lewis puts it, "the road to the Promised Land runs past Mount Sinai." The moral law is a road map, not a home. Our knowledge of God's moral requirements and of our own moral failure, and our repentance, is only the first step, like a doctor's diagnosis of a disease. Then comes the Good News, the prognosis and the prescription, the operation: God's healing, forgiving, and saving us. *That* is why Jesus came to earth: not to preach morality (the prophets had already done that) but to save us by dying and rising. That is the essence of the Christian religion. It begins with morality but it goes far beyond it.

Kierkegaard, the great nineteenth-century Danish Christian existentialist philosopher, distinguished three "stages on life's way." The first was a pre-moral or amoral stage of pleasure-seeking, which he called "aesthetic existence." The second was the moral stage, or "ethical existence," where you judge choices not as pleasant vs. painful, as you did in the "aesthetic stage," but as good vs. evil. But the third and highest stage, the religious stage, is more than and different from the ethical stage just as the ethical is different from the aesthetic. It is a lived relationship with God, not just morality. The aesthetic categories are pleasure vs. pain, the ethical categories are good vs. evil, and the religious categories are sin vs. faith, or life alienated from God vs. life in relationship with God. (Faith is a lived relationship, not just a believed idea.)

If religion were only a means to the end of being moral, we could drop the religious means and just perform the moral end, directly. But religion is not only a means to morality. Religion is an end, not a means. Religion is more than morality. Morality is like a photograph, religion is like the real person in the photograph. Morality is abstract, religion is concrete. Morality gives you Christ-likeness, religion gives you Christ.

Religion is not only more than morality, it may even transcend it, as it did in the case of Abraham and Isaac, which Kierkegaard recounts in *Fear and Trembling.* In order to be religiously faithful, to obey God, Abraham had to do what universal morality forbids: offer up his son Isaac as a holocaust to God, at God's direct command. This is an exceptional case, of course, but it illustrates a general

principle: that real religion is a personal, individual relationship with God, not just an impersonal relationship with
universal moral law.

Since religion is more than morality, you *can* be moral
without being religious, like Socrates and some morally
good agnostics and atheists today.

CAN YOU LIVE A GOOD LIFE WITHOUT LIVING A GODLY LIFE?

The solution to this problem is like the earlier one: we can
know moral goodness without knowing God, but we cannot
really live the good life, the moral life, without living the
divine life.

The good atheist is in fact tapping into God's own life
insofar as he is good. There is no other real source of
goodness than God. If someone disbelieves in God but
nevertheless lives (to some extent) in genuine, unselfish
love (*agape*), then that someone is living in God without
knowing it. This is not my opinion; it is Scripture's clear
teaching: "God is love, and he who abides in love abides in
God, and God abides in him" (1 John 4:16).

This is not necessarily a *saving* "abiding." Perhaps it is,
perhaps it is not. God alone knows our hearts and eternal
destinies. Is the "good atheist" saved? That's for God to
know and for us not to find out, in this life. When the
disciples asked Jesus, "Are many saved?" he replied, "Strive
to enter in." In other words, mind your own business, your
own salvation, rather than speculating about others', which
you don't know.

Justin Martyr, the great second-century Church Father,
wrote that when a pagan like Socrates knew any truth, it
was Christ he knew because Christ is the source of all truth.
Christ is not only the incarnate Jewish carpenter but also the
pre-incarnate universal Logos, or divine mind. "The light

that enlightens every man was coming into the world," according to John 1:9. Augustine said that Christ is the "inner teacher" or "divine illumination" that is the cause or source of every truth that anyone knows, even the atheist. Similarly, whenever a human being, believer or unbeliever, chooses good, he chooses God, whether he knows it or not; and whenever he lives in love, he lives in God, whether he knows it or not.

When the morally good atheist practices Christian morality better than many Christians do, he is not succeeding in being good without God. It's God's grace that's helping him be good, even though he doesn't recognize it or give God the thanks that is due to him for it (Romans 1:21).

You can no more be good without God than you can see without light. But you needn't notice the light when you see objects.

God is the source of all goodness. Moral goodness is like light and God is like the sun. You can see sunlight without seeing the sun, just as an atheist can know moral goodness without knowing God; but there can't really be any sunlight without there being a sun, and there can't really be any moral goodness, even in the life of an atheist, without there really being a good God who is the sole source and first cause of all goodness.

IF YOU CAN BE MORAL WITHOUT BELIEVING IN GOD, WHY BELIEVE?

First of all, because it's true. That's the only honest reason for believing anything. Even if it would make you happy and help you to be a better person if you believed in Santa Claus, you don't. Why? Because you know it isn't true. Truth is an absolute. It can't be manipulated or used for any other purposes.

Second, because God deserves it. God exists and reveals

himself, and once you become aware of that, you also become aware that he deserves your worship. The ultimate reason for belief and love and worship of God is not because of us but because of God.

Third—but only third—because of us. We need an explicit, not just an implicit, knowledge of God, and an explicit, not just an implicit, living in God. A few unusually bright and strong-willed and saintly atheists may be able to live a saintly life without belief in God or turning to God, but for most of us, that is impossible.

The difference religion makes to morality can be seen by comparing anti-drug programs that are not motivated by any religion with those that are. Many secular authorities confess that the only really successful drug rehabilitation programs, the only ones they've ever seen that work really powerfully, are the religious ones.

Think of the hardest moral choice: to endure suffering, torture, and death, to be a martyr. Do you think anyone would do that only for vague, general, philosophical reasons, without a God? Would you be crucified for "morality"? But thousands of ordinary people chose torture and death for Christ, beginning with his own disciples and extending right up to present-day victims of totalitarian regimes.

Without explicit knowlege of God, many great things are still possible, but "with God, *all* things are possible" (Matthew 19:26). We can do many good things without knowing Christ, but "I can do *all* things in him who strengthens me" (Philippians 4:13).

Part Three

Possibilities: Classifying Moral Options

FIVE

Twelve Little Boxes
Morality Won't Fit Into

H AVE YOU EVER WON AN ARGUMENT about morality? Has the other person ever won? Why not? Why do we almost never see any argument about morality resolved? Because most arguments about moral issues turn out to be arguments between two opposite *presuppositions*, or premises. Each of the two arguers is coming from a different starting point, beginning with a different concern. For instance, it may turn out that one is assuming the values of the political Right, the other, that of the Left. Or one is primarily interested in individual ethics, the other in social ethics. Or one is beginning with faith, the other with reason. Or one is thinking of ethics as objective and impersonal, the other as subjective and personal. Or one is treating ethics as a matter of absolutes, the other, as a matter of relativities. Or one sees ethics as conformity to law and the other as a means to enhancing freedom. One is thinking with his head, the other with his heart. One has an ethics of the intellect, the other, of the will. One emphasizes seriousness, the other, joy. One emphasizes law, the other, grace. One emphasizes law, the other, personal character. One emphasizes self, the other, altruism. These are the little boxes that a complete morality is too big to fit into.

No one of these emphases is enough for a complete morality. A complete morality includes and transcends all these pairs of opposites and is not confined to any one of them. Once this "presuppositional" issue is clarified, once this disagreement about "where you're coming from" is cleared up, and not until then, we can see why people usually disagree about moral issues. So the issue of this chapter is really a very practical one, an essential means to the end of understanding each other and resolving moral disputes.

PRINCIPLES OF PROBLEM-SOLVING

Before looking at the twelve little boxes morality won't fit into, we should sharpen the eyes with which we will look, by trying to understand the structure of the problems these little boxes try (unsuccessfully) to solve.

Any problem at all must have the nature of some sort of tension or conflict between two things. If there is only one thing, there is no problem. For instance, Job had no problem with his *faith* in God's justice until his *experience* of apparent injustice (undeserved suffering) seemed to contradict it. Scientists had no problem with light as something made of *waves* until it was discovered that it was also made of *particles*.

So the structure of every problem can be diagrammed as follows:

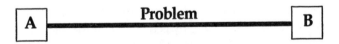

By looking at this common structure of every problem, we can see that there are five possible solutions to any problem:
1. Ignore it. Give up. Hope it will go away. (= no solution at all)

2. Affirm A and ignore B.
3. Affirm B and ignore A.
4. Compromise. Give up a little of A and a little of B. Neither side is completely satisfied.
5. Find a higher, larger solution, C, that includes all the truth in A *and* all the truth in B.

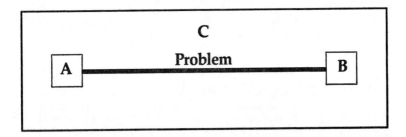

For instance, one of the fundamental problems in politics is the rights of the individual vs. the rights of the state. If we are not going to simply ignore the problem and give up (solution #1), and are not going to simply affirm individual rights and deny the rights of the state (equals anarchy, solution #2), or simply affirm the rights of the state and deny the rights of the individual (equals totalitarianism, solution #3), we have only two solutions left, #4 and #5. Solution #4 is compromise. The state has some authority (*e.g.*, to draft the citizen into the army and compel him to risk his life in war) and the individual has some authority (*e.g.*, to criticize the state, to move away, to possess guns). This (solution #4) is certainly a better solution than the others; but in an ideal state (solution #5) everyone would freely and naturally feel so patriotic that they would identify their own private, individual good very closely with the good of the whole community, and the state would be so concerned with individuals that all of its efforts would be geared to the purpose of helping individuals, not expanding its own power.

In terms of our diagram, this is solution C, the higher point of view—love and cooperation and a kind of family spirit—that does full justice to both halves of the problem, the individual *and* the state.

Another example would be the apparent contradiction between religious faith and modern science. For instance, doesn't Genesis say we were created by God in his image, while modern biology tells us we evolved over a long period of time from apes? The two most popular "solutions" to this problem are #2 and #3 in our list. Believers in evolution often simply scorn or sneer at religious believers, and believers in creation often ignore the scientific data rather than explaining it. But a better solution (C in our diagram) would be a larger, more complete one. What the Bible tells us is that the soul was created by God, breathed into us by God. That is "the image of God"—the soul. What the theory of evolution (and it is only a theory) supposes is that the human body gradually evolved from the higher apes, as they evolved from more primitive apes, which in turn evolved from more primitive life forms, etc. Now perhaps the theory is simply wrong scientifically; but if it is right, it does not contradict the biblical account because it says nothing at all about the soul. How could science see souls? Are there fossils of souls embedded in rocks? God *could* have gradually prepared the human body by evolution and then created the soul and breathed it into the body. That would be a more complete, two-part explanation, including both body and soul. C includes both A and B.

There is no need to box ourselves into a corner, to crawl into the little box that is only half the picture. Most problems can be solved by raising our sights and including without compromise whatever truth is to be found in each of the two competing halves of the whole picture. For even though these two parts of the problem apparently contradict each other, truth can never contradict truth. Therefore whatever is true in A and B can be reconciled in C. Arguments can be resolved by both sides raising their sights and refusing to be confined to little boxes.

The twelve little boxes that confine most people's morality today are:

1. the Right vs. the Left
2. the individual vs. society
3. faith vs. reason
4. the objective vs. the subjective
5. the absolute vs. the relative
6. conformity vs. freedom
7. head vs. heart
8. intellect vs. will
9. seriousness vs. joy
10. law vs. grace
11. impersonal laws vs. personal character
12. egoism vs. altruism

THE BOX OF RIGHT VERSUS LEFT

The two most popular little boxes for thinking about nearly everything today are the ideological boxes of Right and Left, or Conservative and Liberal, or Traditional and Progressive. In a politicized country, where the real religion of many people is politics, where religion is treated politically and politics is treated religiously, Right and Left are the two most popular fishnets to try to contain all the fish that the mind can catch. The media habitually look at all things in these categories, and so do the increasing number of people who let the media do their thinking for them.

Classifying every idea as "left" or "right" saves wear and tear on the brain. It saves you from having to do the hard work of thinking through each question on its own. For some people, "conservative" or "old" is simply a synonym for "false"; for others, it is simply a synonym for "true." It's much easier, you see, to tell the truth with a clock than with a thought; to ask "is it new?" instead of "is it true?"

If you classify yourself as either Liberal or Conservative, see how you react to the following descriptions. Liberals describe conservatism as hard-headed, legalistic, impersonal, rigid, self-righteous, pugnacious, and militaristic. Conservatives describe liberalism as soft-headed, spineless, wimpy, compromising, indulgent, pandering, permissive, and unprincipled. Liberals accuse Conservatives of having lost their heart, their compassion, and Conservatives accuse Liberals of having lost their mind.

If you are a Liberal, you probably think the above description of Conservatives is accurate (that's why you're not one) but the description of Liberals is not (that's why you are one). If you are a Conservative, you probably think the above description of Liberals is accurate (that's why you're not one) but the description of Conservatives is not (that's why you are one).

Perhaps *both* sides are missing something.

The strategy behind liberalism was to win the world by compassion, by universal agreement, by compromise. But it will never work, because no one buys a product unless it's *better* than its competitors. To endlessly water down and compromise all principles for the sake of being acceptable is to become unacceptable. It is our old "Principle of First and Second Things." Give up the truth for the sake of selling it, and you won't even sell it.

The strategy behind conservatism was the opposite: hold the line, fight the good fight, keep the faith. But suppose the faith, and the truth, is not the kind of thing that can be won by fighting, and not even the kind of thing that can be *kept* by force, or by grasping it tightly? Then conservatism has failed to conserve. Politically, it has not conserved the environment, or the small things of the past in its support of big business. "Small is beautiful" should be a conservative slogan, but it is Liberals who usually praise Schumacher's great little book by that title.

When it comes to moral issues about human life, Liberals

are strangely willing to sacrifice the lives of the innocent (especially the old and the unborn) but not the guilty (the murderer on death row or the soldier of an aggressive enemy). Conservatives tend to the opposite selective morality, opposing abortion and euthanasia but eager to keep guns, capital punishment, and military force as the quick-fix solution to international problems. I have never understood how the sacred absolute of life becomes a secular relativity just because it changes its address from a battlefield to an abortion clinic or vice versa.

The saints transcend these two little illogical boxes. They are consistently moral, consistently reverential toward all human lives, and therefore they get in trouble with both Left and Right. Just as Jesus did. The Pharisees were the Right of his time and the Sadducees were the Left. They agreed about nothing except him. Jesus didn't buy into their little boxes. He was dangerously big.

The New Testament does not lay down a detailed blueprint for a Christian society, either a Left one or a Right one. Yet it gives us enough hints to transcend and offend both little boxes. There is an emphasis on charity, a "preferential option for the poor," a condemnation of private and public greed, and even a voluntary socialism-communism of property. On the other hand, there is an equally strong emphasis on authority, obedience, and tradition, on fidelity, family, and work, and on theological orthodoxy. No one of the typical American Left or Right can read all this without feeling uncomfortable. Of course. As Chesterton says, there is one angle at which you stand upright, many opposite angles at which you fall—to the left or to the right. If the New Testament is indeed divine revelation, the mind of God, then we should expect the mind of man to naturally depart from this in opposite ways. When the human train has gone off the divine track in both directions, the track will seem threatening to both parts of the train in opposite ways.

One of the secrets of the saints, as opposed to the Left and the Right, is suffering. Saints put themselves on the line. They don't just argue, they offer themselves up for others, as Jesus did. That's why Joan Andrews in jail has a power to stop abortion that politicians and philosophers don't have, and why Ghandi, fasting, stopped the British army as guns could not. Little boxes are safe. Following Christ is not safe. His promise is: "In the world you will have tribulation." When you don't crawl into the world's little boxes, you suffer. That's the bad news. The good news follows: "But be of good cheer; I have overcome the world."

When making moral choices, the only consideration is to make the right choice, not the Right choice or the Left choice. The world invented Left and Right; God invented right. We American conformists are tempted, more than people in most other societies, to let our world, our society, do our thinking for us.

But we are commanded:

> Do not be conformed to this world, but be transformed by the renewal of your mind, that you may prove what is the will of God, what is good and acceptable and perfect.
> (Romans 12:2)

That is the rule for Christian moral decision-making.

THE BOX OF INDIVIDUAL VERSUS SOCIAL

There is a "soft," or inexact, but not a "hard," or exact, match between the Right and ethical individualism, and between the Left and ethical socialism. The tension between the private good and the public or common good is a frequent source of disagreement about moral issues. One party will look at the issue from the individual point of view, the other from the social; or one party will specialize in social issues (like poverty), the other in individual issues (like abortion). The Right tend to an individualistic ethic and religion and the Left tends to the "social gospel."

But you can't specialize in virtue. You can't be a complete individual without a social conscience, *and* you can't have a good society unless it is built of the building blocks of good individuals. For both war and peace begin right here at home, in the individual human hearts.

THE BOX OF FAITH VERSUS REASON

Some find their morality by faith, some by reason. Some see morality as dependent simply on the will of God, which we know only by faith. Others see it as dependent on the divine *reason,* or human reason and human nature. (This is similar to the issue dealt with in Chapter Four, the foundation of moral absolutes.)

The answer, as usual, is both. In practice, a morality not informed and corrected by divine revelation will always have blind spots. In theory, the moral thing is always the truly reasonable thing. In practice, ethics without religion is nearly impossible. In theory, it is possible because knowledge of right and wrong does not depend on religious faith. Each side has a point but usually fails to admit each other's point.

THE BOX OF OBJECTIVE VERSUS SUBJECTIVE, OR IMPERSONAL VERSUS PERSONAL

Closely connected to the last issue is this one: Is ethics a universal science or a personal art? Is it a matter of laws and values that hold for everyone, just as the laws of mathematics do? Or is it an art, a habit, almost a knack, that the saints have as part of their personal character and that unholy people simply don't have? Anyone can learn arithmetic, but some people can do yoga more easily than others. Is morality more like arithmetic or more like yoga?

The principles themselves are more like arithmetic, but living them is more like yoga. The "objectivist" is usually thinking of the laws, principles, rights, and ideals when he says ethics is objective, and the "subjectivist" is thinking of the need for the individual to internalize these when he says ethics is subjective. Objective principles are useless unless we subjectively live them. It is a silly dispute; both are right and both are needed. But again, both often fail to see the point of the other.

THE BOX OF ABSOLUTE VERSUS RELATIVE

In light of our defense of moral absolutes in Chapter Three, it may surprise the reader to see relativity defended here as the other half of a valid moral dualism. But remember our three moral factors: the moral quality of the act itself, which is objective and absolute; the motive, which is subjective and absolute; and the circumstances, or situation, which is objective and relative. The situation is always an ingredient in a moral choice; therefore there is always a relative ingredient in a moral choice.

The relativist, however, gets things backwards. He thinks there are no absolutes because he takes his guidance from the situation instead of from principles. The simple, mere absolutist makes the opposite mistake: he forgets that absolute principles must be applied relative to changing situations. The relativist emphasizes changing applications and has no unchanging principles to apply; the mere absolutist or legalist emphasizes unchanging principles and forgets that they must be applied. The whole point of principles is to apply them, but the whole point of applying them is that you apply *principles*. It is like faith and works: just as principles without application is dead, "faith without works is dead." Equally, works without faith are dead, like applications without principles.

THE BOX OF CONFORMITY VERSUS FREEDOM

Is morality a matter of conforming to principles or ideals, bowing down before something outside of me, putting myself second? Or is it putting my true self first and attaining freedom and liberation? Do I exist for principles or do principles exist for me?

On the one hand, unless principles are above me and commanding me, and unless I must conform to them, there *are* no principles, only "good advice." On the other hand, principles are for us, not us for principles. "The sabbath was made for man, not man for the sabbath" (Mark 2:27).

What then is supposed to be the primary purpose of my ethical effort and striving and faithfulness: obedience or freedom? Conformity or liberation?

It is another false dilemma, for conforming to true ethical principles is the only way to true liberation. "The truth will make you free" (John 8:32). A ballet dancer becomes free to make beautiful moves only by conforming herself to laws and principles in disciplined practice. A scholar becomes free from ignorance only by conforming to truth, to data, to facts.

I am not called to be merely faithful to principles, nor merely faithful to persons, but faithful to persons via principles. Principles (like "thou shalt not commit adultery") are the formula for fidelity to persons. The way to freedom (from sin, death, suffering, betrayal, evil of all kinds) is by conformity and obedience to the divine law. Aspiring to freedom without conformity to principles is self-destructive. No one is ever freed by trampling on the very road map of freedom, the very way to freedom. On the other hand, all the laws we must conform to are only means to the end of personal liberation from evil.

We all know, from experience, the illusion of false freedom that comes from breaking out of the bonds imposed on us by moral law. We all know that first, false feeling of freedom: it seems as if we entered a larger, more perilous but more interesting world by eating some forbidden fruit. But it is a lie, the same lie our ancestors fell for in Eden. The "larger" world of disobedience turns out to be confining and small and unfree. The criminal or the addict lives in a tiny world; the saint lives in the larger world. Evil looks large and interesting and perilous from afar, but it reveals its true colors from nearby or from within, from experience: tiny and tawdry.

Not many writers tell the truth here. Modern writers usually miss what Hannah Arendt, in *Eichmann in Jerusalem*, calls "the banality of evil." How large and interesting the Nazis seem from afar! How many movies and novels have been written about them, romanticizing and glorifying their apparently fascinating evil? But they were really shrunken souls, gray, dull little constricted selves.

Writers can be classified on a spectrum according to how well they see this truth that morality is freeing and immorality confining. At the lowest extreme is Nietzsche and his followers, like Hesse, whose characters are imprisoned by their dilemma of immoral freedom vs. moral conformity. At the opposite extreme are writers like C.S. Lewis, Charles Williams, and J.R.R. Tolkien, who portray the good-evil conflict (which is the substance of every story in some way) as it really is; they show good as more interesting than evil, not vice versa. The primary reason so few writers are on their end of the spectrum and so many on Nietzsche's end is the false dilemma of conformity vs. freedom.

The root of this, in turn, is usually the fallacy that "conformity" means conformity to *society*, to man-made laws rather than conformity to natural law, which is God-made, objective, unchangeable, and universal. It is the denial of these moral absolutes that is at the root of the attack on conformity, reducing conformity to a sociological pattern of action or a psychological habit of feeling—conformity to society rather than to truth.

THE BOX OF HEAD VERSUS HEART

Do we make moral decisions by reason (the head) or by feeling, instinct, intuition (heart, in the modern sense)? The classical tradition says the former, the romantic and modern tradition says the latter.

"Star Wars" is an example of the latter. Luke Skywalker has to shut his eyes and "trust the Force." But books on morality, including this one, and moral institutions such as think tanks, college ethics courses, and political bureaucracies that are entrusted with decision-making, by the mere fact that they are structured and planned, presuppose the other answer: that we must make the right decisions by thinking about them. If instinct and intuition were sufficient, we would not need all these aids to thought.

But without moral instinct, the human race could never have made moral decisions and regulated its life morally. If we had no instinct to serve others, we would never have developed social structures of any kind. If our hearts did not bleed for the innocent victim, our heads would never have invented police. Moral thought can only be an aid to moral instinct, never a substitute for it.

The answer to the head-heart dualism is obvious in theory: we need to use both, not just one. But in practice that is difficult.

One of the reasons it is especially difficult today is that the modern world has narrowed the meanings of both head and heart, thus making it harder for them to come together. What we mean by "reason" is usually taken from the model of science: analytic, logical, calculative reasoning based on empirical data. But what the ancients meant by "reason" was much broader than that. It included wisdom and understanding and insight and intellectual intuition— something closer to what we would call the heart.

On the other hand, we have also narrowed and constricted the meaning of "heart." Scripture (and writers like Augustine) use it to mean the center of a person's whole being; the spirit, or I, or self that stands beneath and behind all the distinguishable functions such as thinking, feeling, and choosing. But we moderns usually mean by "heart" only "feeling." What's the difference? The "heart" which is the center of your being has an eye in it; the "heart" which is only your feelings does not.

Thus what the ancients meant by "reason" and what they meant by "heart" were very close. To unify these two in practice, we must unify them in our understanding first, and to do that we must read and recapture the vision of the ancients, starting with Scripture.

THE BOX OF INTELLECT VERSUS WILL

This duality is close to but not exactly the same as head vs. heart. The issue here is not so much how we *see* moral truth, with reason or with intuition; but the *relation* between seeing (or knowing) and choosing (or willing). We make choices with our will; the question here is, should the will always follow the intellect?

If the *intellect* is closer to the center of our being, if it is the highest or deepest thing in us, then the answer is yes, the will should always follow the intellect. If the *will* is closer to our center, our very self, then the answer is no.

But when it comes to understanding *persons* rather than *things* in nature, the will should lead the mind. The only way to really know persons is to love them. Thus Jesus tells those who misunderstood his teaching that their mistake was rooted in their will, not their mind: "If your will were to do the will of my Father, you would understand my teaching, that it is from him" (John 7:17).

So which is first? Is the intellect the root of the will or vice versa? Does the intellect move and determine the will, or vice versa? Both. The intellect gives direction, moral maps, and information to the will. Without the intellect, the will is blind. But the will is the master, captain, and ruler of the mind. We can will our mind to look or not to look, and the will also can choose to obey or disobey what the mind shows us. Once again, the answer is a both/and rather than an either/or. The mind is the navigator, the will is the captain.

Applied to practical moral choices, this means that the mere intellectual and the anti-intellectual are both wrong. When someone makes a bad moral choice, the fault is with both the mind and the will, not with one alone.

One ingredient of every bad choice is ignorance. If the thief only knew, really knew, realized to the depth of his being, that stealing could not bring him happiness, that moral goodness is always more profitable to him than moral evil, then he would have no motive to be a thief.

But on the other hand, the root of this *ignorance* is willful *ignoring*. To be a thief you must first voluntarily blind yourself to the moral facts. The pleasure you hope to derive from your stolen money beckons you from one direction; and the truth of the moral law, the truth that evil can never make you really happy in the long run, shines on you from the other direction; and your will must *choose to look* in one direction or the other.

So the will directs the reason, *and* the reason directs the will. Both must be addressed; both must work; both must be straightened out, if we are to make moral choices rightly.

THE BOX OF SERIOUS VERSUS JOYFUL

Some people take morality so seriously that there is no room for joy. Others insist that joy is the final end and refuse to take morality with absolute seriousness. Both see something. And both miss something.

The very dualism between the serious and the joyful is a mistake. Most people today cannot be serious and joyful at the same time. To be serious, to them, is to be *deadly* serious, fixed of jaw and stiffened of muscle, not relaxed, and therefore not joyful. On the other hand, their idea of joy is a vacation, a relief, an oasis from the desert of "real life" seriousness.

In the Bible, especially the Psalms, you find a very different attitude. The psalmist is most joyful precisely when he takes God most seriously. The "weightiest" matters— God, God's law, God's purposes—bring him the most joy. He rejoices not in a vacation from reality but in ultimate reality, in God. For the heaviest thing, the absolute reality, is also the lightest thing, the most joyful thing.

Morality is not the joyless thing it seems to most moderns. True morality is ultimately to will as God wills, and if God is the source of joy as well as the source of moral law, then it should be natural for us to *delight* in the law, as the psalmist does: "O how I love thy law!/It is my meditation all the day" (Psalm 119:97). If we don't understand that, it will be hard for us to be moral, because (as Thomas Aquinas observes, profoundly) "no man can live without joy. Therefore if he lacks spiritual [true] joy, he will necessarily turn to carnal [false] joys" (*Summa Theologica* I-II, 35, 4). The only antidote to the attractiveness of immorality is a morality that is even more attractive.

THE BOX OF LAW VERSUS GRACE

This is mainly, but not exclusively, a Protestant-Catholic conflict. Protestantism was born with Luther's rediscovery that we are "not under law but under grace" (Romans 6:14). Catholic language, on the other hand, speaks of the gospel as the "new law." We seem to have here a genuine conflict between a morality that takes its bearings from grace and the inspirations of the Spirit within, freed from the law and a morality that insists that the Commandments are binding for all ages including our own (because God's Word is unchangeable).

As usual, Thomas Aquinas helps with some necessary distinctions. We are freed from the *curse* of the law but not from the *obligation* to obey it. We are freed (by grace) from the *punishment* due to our disobedience (that is how we are "not under the law but under grace"), we are *saved* by grace. That is Catholic as well as Protestant teaching, strongly reaffirmed by the Council of Trent. Our sins are forgiven. But they are still sins, and we know this only by the law (Romans 3:20).

The practical issue is this: When a Christian makes a moral decision, should he or she look at the Commandments or look to the grace of the Holy Spirit? Again, the answer must be both. The Commandments are the road map, the Spirit's grace is the fuel. Looking only to the law and not to divine grace means we will not have the grace even to understand the meaning of the law and how it is to be applied to our situation, and also that we will not have the power to obey it. But looking to grace only and not to law at all means we will be prone to all sorts of excesses of individualism and "enthusiasm" (in the sense Ronald Knox used in his classic by that title). All heretics in history appealed to grace, the Spirit, and inner inspiration, and ignored the objective data of divine revelation, the law and words of Scripture and the teaching church.

As we shall see in a later chapter, to make moral choices we must "line up" or triangulate three factors: the objective moral law, the situation which God's providence brings us to, and the Spirit's grace in our hearts. The moral tripod cannot stand on two legs.

THE BOX OF LAW VERSUS CHARACTER

A related but different issue is: Do we take our guidance from our duties and rights as specified by moral law, or by the inner habits of character, the virtues? Is morality primarily a matter of determining justice, right, duty, and law, as it is in most modern ethical discussion? Or is it primarily a matter of personal virtues vs. vices, building good rather than bad character, as it is in most classical ethics? Should we make moral road maps and trust that moral travelers will learn how to become good travelers? Or should we train good travelers and trust that they will find their own way?

The answer is that we need both, of course. Because most modern morality is so concerned with social issues, individual character, virtues and vices, tend to be ignored today. But a society built of morally bad or immature individuals cannot be a good society. A wall built of weak bricks must be a weak wall. And what makes good bricks, or good individuals, are the moral virtues. So defining and fostering the virtues must be a primary and essential task of any morality.

But we cannot simply rely on virtuous individuals to find their way without moral maps. We need to find what are the right and wrong roads (objective laws), as well as what are the good and bad vehicles (personal virtues). A broken-down vehicle won't go anywhere, no matter how good the maps. But the best vehicle will get lost without maps.

THE BOX OF EGOISM VERSUS ALTRUISM

Obviously, we cannot be egotists and moral at the same time. The most basic and generally acknowledged principle of all morality is to overcome egotism (selfishness). But egoism is not the same as egotism. Egoism says the self is a rightful end, a rightful object of concern; that the end of morality is self-fulfillment. Altruism says we should be self-forgetful and seek the good of others, not of self. Is a concern for our own happiness the rightful end of morality or not?

It is *a* rightful end but not *the* rightful end. Again, we need both. Being moral is the only way to personal happiness, and we should know this all-important fact because God designed us to have a natural regard for our own welfare. Jesus commanded us to love our neighbor *as ourselves,* not instead of ourselves. Seeking our own happiness is not bad; it is good.

But the only way to be happy is to be good, and the only way to be good (to yourself) is to be good to others, even to the extent of self-sacrifice. As the supreme moral teacher put it, "he who loses his life for my sake will find it" (Matthew 10:39).

Self and other are locked in metaphysical marriage; neither can be perfected without the other. God made us essentially social creatures, so that our own and our neighbor's happiness could not be separated and opposed, except by moral blindness. We are related organically, like organs in a body, not like two people on opposite ends of a seesaw.

Most (but not quite all) of these twelve issues are part of

the current Right-Left specialization. Thus the Right specializes in individual ethics, the Left in social; the Right in religion, the Left in reason; the Right in the objective, the Left in the subjective; the Right in absolutes, the Left in relativities; the Right in conformity, the Left in freedom; the Right in the head, the Left in the heart. If we free ourselves from the webs of the world's confining categories, we will go far toward overcoming many moral dilemmas. Whatever true morality *is* (and we have not yet by any means given an adequate answer to that question), we should know clearly twelve little-box things it *isn't.*

SIX

Ten Candidates for the Greatest Good: Your Scale of Values

E VERY GREAT PHILOSOPHER has philosophized about it. Every great writer has written about it. Every thoughtful person has thought about it. And every active person has acted on it. It is the quest for the *summum bonum*, the greatest good, the ultimate meaning and purpose of life, the answer to the question: Why was I born? Why am I living?

Even the shallow and skeptical technique of "values clarification" so popular today in many schools raises this great question. Students are asked to "clarify their values" by confronting moral dilemmas such as these: If you were a captain on a life raft with three other people—an evil philanthropist, a retarded child, and the President—and there was only enough food for two to survive, what would you do? If a museum was burning and you had time to save either the Mona Lisa or an old, dying janitor, which would you save? Would you change jobs if it meant quadrupling your salary but halving your time with your family? Would you tell a lie to avoid hurting someone's feelings?

All these questions require you to use a scale or hierarchy of values in choosing one of two courses of action. Which value comes first? What are your priorities? What is the greatest good?

It is a legitimate question, though it is misused in "values clarification" in two ways. First, the situational moral dilemmas are posed in a purely relativistic and subjectivistic way, as if there were no right or wrong answers, as if your choice of values were like your choice of clothes. Second, the impression is sometimes left that unusual moral dilemmas like the lifeboat or the burning museum make up the whole of morality, or at least its central part. But the abuse does not take away the proper use. The question of moral priorities, the hierarchy of goods, and the greatest good at the top remains useful.

Here are four reasons why the question of the greatest good is useful, even necessary.

1. It is *basic*. It is not the *only* moral question, but it is the *first* one. All moral choices presuppose some answer to it, so it is logically first. Every step along our road is directed to our end.

It is also *psychologically* first, for you can understand it even when you are very young. I think the day I first became a philosopher was when I understood this question and found it thrilling. I was about eight, and heard a sermon on Ecclesiastes (which is about exactly that question) which (to my amazement) I could understand and (even more amazing) did not bore me but excited me. I was not unusually precocious; any child can participate in this quest for the end or meaning of life.

2. It is *ultimate*. Though basic and simple, the question is at the same time the most profound, the most important of all questions. Answering it is the ultimate choice each of us makes; the choice of our life's ultimate end, meaning, point, purpose, good, goal, guide, and value. How wonderful that the simplest thing should be also the ultimate thing, and that the ultimate thing should be also the simplest!

3. It is *universal.* It affects everything. All choices implicitly presuppose it. Here's why. You choose one thing rather than another only because you think it is *better* in some way, it has more good, or value. Now there are two kinds of good: means and ends. Means are good for something else, ends are good for themselves. Medicines, tools, money, cars, books, buildings, and foods are means. Truth, beauty, love, and pleasure are ends. And the question of the final end is universal because the end justifies all the means.

A specific end does not necessarily justify a specific means, because even a good end does not justify an evil means. The good end of feeding the poor does not justify the evil means of killing the rich. But a good end justifies a good means. What else could? Why take medicine except for the end of health? Why read books except for the end of knowledge, or pleasure?

Since the good end justifies the good means, the ultimate end, or the greatest good, justifies every choice of good means to it, just as the home at the end of the road justifies every step you take toward it.

4. Above all, it is a *practical* question. For without a hierarchy of values with a highest value at the top, a choice between higher goods and lower goods can't be intelligently made. Unless you know your end, you can't know what means get you there.

The choice between good and evil presents no problem to *thought,* only to action. You need a good *will* to choose good. But you need a good *mind* to *know* good. That's the purpose of this book. The puzzling choice is the choice between two goods. For that, you need a scale of values, with the greatest good or ultimate purpose of life at the top.

The choice between two goods is like the choice between two friends. Though you value both, you have only a finite amount of time, and you have to choose sometimes which one to spend your time with.

Preferring one good to another is not treating the lesser good as bad, any more than choosing to spend time with one friend rather than another is treating the other as an enemy. Saving the janitor instead of the Mona Lisa from the museum fire is not treating the Mona Lisa as trash.

We should never act *against* a good, but we may and must *ignore* a good sometimes to do another good. For example, destroying a marriage is wrong, but not getting married so as to devote your whole life to some other good thing is not wrong.

Morality means choice. Choice means priorities. Priorities mean a hierarchy. A hierarchy means something at the top, a standard. That is the greatest good. If you have no greatest good, you have no hierarchy of goods. If you have no hierarchy, you have no priorities. If you have no priorities, you cannot make intelligent choices. If you cannot make intelligent moral choices, you have no morality.

You can still guide your life by your feelings or by social fashions, but that is not choice—not free, responsible, moral choice. Both feelings and fashions push you; you are passive. But moral choice is your own doing; you are active. You are responsible for your choices but not for your feelings or for your environment's fashions.

Feelings and fashions are relative to each other. They are two aspects of the same worldly order. They are like money and power: each can buy the other. Fashions are the social form taken by the feelings of the fashion-makers, and feelings are the psychological form taken by social fashions. For example, most men today feel attracted to thin women because that is the fashion in our society (it was not so in the Renaissance); and that is the fashion in our society because that is how fashion-makers feel.

The choice, then, is not between going by your internal feelings or by external fashions. Feelings may seem individual, even nonconformist, but they are conditioned by social fashions. The only real choice comes when you rise from the level of feelings and fashions to the level of free will and moral values. Only a choice between right and wrong is *your* choice; a choice between a big car and a small car in response to advertisements is really society's choice.

The question of the greatest good is a practical question above all because it is much like the sailing orders of a fleet of ships. (The metaphor comes from C.S. Lewis.) The ships need to know three things. First, the fleet must know how to cooperate, how to avoid getting in each other's way. That is like social ethics: justice and peace and charity. Second, each ship has to know how to stay shipshape and seaworthy. That is like individual ethics: virtues and vices. Social goodness depends on individual goodness because you can no more make a good society out of bad individuals than you can make a good team out of bad players. Third, and most important, the fleet must know its mission. Why is it at sea in the first place? What is the end to which everything else in the first two categories is a means? That is the question of the greatest good.

Modern morality usually concentrates on social ethics, tends to forget individual ethics, and almost always ignores the question of the greatest good of all. Why? I think there are two reasons. First, there is much agreement about social ethics and much disagreement about the greatest good. And our egalitarian society fears real disagreement, especially about ultimate values. Second, religion answers the question of the greatest good, and modern society fears religion and tries to keep it private and out of public life. So the ultimate question, the greatest good, is relegated to private, subjective feelings. Belief in God is treated in the same way as a headache, or a taste for olives.

That, by the way, is the basic reason why secular societies are dying. A society can no more survive without an ultimate reason for living than an individual can.

AN OBVIOUS ANSWER

But isn't this question of identifying the greatest good so ultimate, so profound, that we mere mortals can hardly dare hope to find the answer? Isn't the truffle too well hidden? Modern skepticism is very dogmatic in assuming so. But instead of being dogmatically skeptical, we should be truly skeptical, *i.e.*, skeptical also of skepticism, fully open-minded. If we are, we will find at least one obvious answer, and that will put us on the road to more.

The answer is *happiness*. As Aristotle discovered long ago, *everyone* loves and seeks and pursues and desires *everything* they love or seek or pursue or desire for one and the same reason: because they hope it will make them happy. Happiness is the end everyone does in fact seek all the time.

This is evident in any example. No one takes bitter medicine, or a painful operation, unless they think it will heal them, and they will be happier healed than sick. No one works hard to make a profit, or a boat, or a victory, unless they think it will make them happy. Even working for others' happiness is the thing that makes the altruist *happy*. Even the suicidal person is motivated by the desire to escape unhappiness. Happy people do not commit suicide.

Not only do we seek all that we seek for the sake of happiness; we also never seek happiness for the sake of any further end. We play ball because it makes us happy, but we do not seek happiness in order to play ball. People often say, "What good is money? It can't buy happiness." But no one says, "What good is happiness? It can't buy money." (Perhaps they do say that in our crazy world.)

So our greatest good is happiness. However, that does not settle much, for a second question arises: what constitutes happiness? What makes it up? What is its content?

One easy answer to this latter question is simply "different strokes for different folks." Whatever turns you on is happiness for you. Happiness is "different things for different people."

This is obviously true on one level: opera makes you happy but not me, chant makes me happy but not you. That's fine as long as all you mean by happiness is the private feeling of satisfaction within the individual's emotions. But how can *that* be the greatest good? Suppose someone gets more satisfaction from making mud pies than from relating to people: does that make mud pies really his greatest good? Wouldn't it be better *for him*, wouldn't it make *him happier*, to learn to relate to people, to love? Doesn't love give greater and truer happiness than making mud pies, even if one person thinks otherwise? Or suppose someone gets satisfaction only from cruelty; does that make cruelty really good? Can we turn evil into good just by liking it?

Some would say yes. They would say that happiness is totally subjective and relative to your desires: no matter what you desire, if only your desire is satisfied, that's all happiness is. But we all know this is not true. We all commonsensically distinguish between real and apparent happiness, true and false happiness. A temporary "high" caused by a mind-destroying drug is not true happiness but false, pseudo-happiness. Satisfaction of the desire for personal revenge is not true happiness on a par with satisfaction of the desire for objective justice.

So we still need to know what *real* or *true* happiness is. We can't assume that our feelings will infallibly tell us because our feelings are not infallible. You can feel quite healthy but really be dying. Or you can feel terribly sick but really be quite healthy. Similarly, you can feel very happy and yet be dying inside, dying in your soul, dying to your humanity. Or you could feel like a failure when in fact you are really a spiritual success and a hero, like Job. Your inner feelings are no more infallible than your outer feelings.

But if our feelings of happiness are fallible, they can be wrong. And if they can be wrong, there must be something for them to be wrong about, some real happiness that they fail to exhibit. In other words, happiness is not just a subjective feeling but an objective state. We must, therefore, find out what constitutes this objective state of *true* happiness.

WHAT IS TRUE HAPPINESS?

We can be aided on our quest if we first classify different *kinds* of answers to this question, just as we can be aided to choose a career or a meal if we first confront the more general question of the *type* of career or meal we want. What types of answers are there to the question of happiness?

Aristotle classified answers in terms of the three types of life he saw people living, the three basic kinds of values people usually devote their lives to. There was first the life of the mind, knowledge (philosophy, science, scholarship). This includes pursuits as diverse as mathematics and mysticism. Second, there was the active life, the pursuit of honor and public service. This includes pursuits as diverse as doctor (professional healer) and mercenary soldier (professional killer). The third is the life of personal gratification, pleasure-seeking. This includes pursuits as diverse as art collecting and gluttony.

Hinduism also has a classification of goods, called the Four Wants of Man. Based on millennia of experience, Hinduism identifies four basic kinds of desires and pursuits (lifestyles, to use the fashionable expression).

First comes the pursuit of *pleasure*. This is natural for youth. There is even a religious erotic love manual to use in this stage, the *Kama Sutra*. At the end, you are bored and seek further stages.

The second goal is wealth and *power*. This is a natural goal for someone in the prime of life. The caste system was originally designed partly to help people structure this desire.

Third comes *altruism,* or social service, once power proves as vain as pleasure. Instead of gathering goods for yourself, you now share them with others. But even this is inadequate because the only goods you know to share so far are the two toys of pleasure and power.

A fourth stage is necessary, and that is the search for Brahman, which is *sat* (infinite reality), *chit* (infinite understanding), and *ananda* (infinite joy), the three divine attributes and the three deepest desires of the human heart.

Kierkegaard classifies all human values under the three categories of aesthetic (self-satisfaction), ethical (duty), and religious (a living relationship with God). Chapter Five reviews and uses his classification.

Freud classifies answers in terms of the problems, which he says are three: relations with nature, with society, and with yourself. To conquer "the superior power of nature," we use science and technology, knowledge and power. To improve "the inadequate relations between people," we use law and order, love and work, family and state. To heal the inner contradiction in the self between the *id* (animal desires) and the super-ego (societal restrictions), Freud invents psychoanalysis. But he says we can never wholly resolve these conflicts, and can never be wholly happy.

The common principle of these and other classifications of ends is that we seek many different ends. We must decide which must be subordinated to which, which is higher. Thus we need a hierarchy, an "order of love," as Augustine puts it. And a hierarchy presupposes not just a higher but a highest. Thus arises the question of the highest good.

TEN CANDIDATES FOR THE GREATEST GOOD

Throughout time and space, among different cultures and different thinkers, ten basic answers to the question of the greatest good have appeared, ten candidates for happiness. As in most elections, there are also minor, fringe candidates running, but few people vote for them. For example, a few people try to find meaning in life by things like hopping on one foot longer than anyone in history, thus making it into *The Guinness Book of World Records*. But the vast majority vote for one of ten candidates. Here is the list. (The second five are, roughly, spiritual equivalents of the first five.)

1. pleasure (pleasing yourself)
2. money (helping yourself to wealth)
3. health
4. honor, fame, glory, acceptance (others' knowledge of you)
5. power ("playing God")
6. peace, contentment
7. altruism (helping others)
8. virtue (health of soul)
9. wisdom (*your* knowledge of truth)
10. God

Pleasure can be either positive or negative (avoiding pain).

Money can be either pursued as an end (hoarding) or a means (spending, shopping).

Health can be either quantitative (a long life) or qualitative (a robust life).

Honor can be due to either your superiority (sought mainly by the ancients) or your sameness and equality (sought mainly by the moderns).

Power can be sought either over nature (by technology) or over people (by either force or persuasion).

Peace can be either peace with self or peace with others.

Altruism can be pursued either as the final end or as a consequence of a further end (*e.g.*, in obedience to God).

Virtue can be either self-regarding and self-righteous or self-forgetful and spontaneous.

Wisdom can be either theoretical (philosophy) or practical (experience).

Finally, God can be pursued either abstractly, in one or more of his attributes (truth, goodness, beauty) or concretely and personally (the relationship meant by "religion").

We must evaluate the credentials of each candidate before we elect one of them to be the ruler of our lives. We want to (1) look at the strongest argument *for* each one, (2) refute that argument, if possible, and also (3) find the strongest argument *against* each candidate. We will be able to refute each one except the last.

(By the way, refuting an *argument for* a candidate is not the same as refuting *the candidate*. We need to do both.)

PLEASURE

The main reason why pleasure seems to be the greatest good and the meaning of happiness is Freud's simple reason: everyone always seeks it, and as an end, never as a means—just as we said about happiness. No one seeks pleasure as a means to wealth, or health, or power, but people seek these other things because they give them pleasure.

But this argument does not prove pleasure *is* happiness. The fact that pleasure is *like* happiness in being an end rather than a means does not prove that pleasure is *identical* with happiness. In fact, the reason pleasure is never sought as a means is that it is a by-product or consequence of happiness—a sort of spillover. Wherever the end of happiness is attained, pleasure attends it. But the reverse is not true: that whenever there is any kind of pleasure, there is true happiness.

The argument *against* pleasure is simple. We are looking for the end *for human beings,* the fulfillment of our humanity, the distinctively human end. But pleasure is not a distinctively human end; we share it with animals. It fulfills our animal part, the body with its desires and emotions, but not our distinctively human part, the soul, including mind and conscience and the deeper desires of the heart that no animal shares.

MONEY

The argument for money as the *summum bonum* is simply that everyone wants it because it can be exchanged for a million different things. It is the universal medium of exchange. Money can buy everything that money can buy.

But that does not prove money is the greatest good. Just because nearly everyone pursues it, that doesn't mean it is worth pursuing; nearly everyone may be foolish. And although it can buy a million *things* it can't buy happiness because happiness is not a *thing*. Money can buy everything money can buy, but it can't buy anything money can't buy.

The reason money can't possibly be our final end is that it is a *means* of exchange, a means to a further end. The greatest good is our ultimate *end*.

HEALTH

"If you have your health, you have everything." Don't many people say this? We would gladly exchange everything for our health. We pay doctors our entire savings to heal us, if necessary.

But not everyone says, "If you have your health, you have everything"—only the old, or people whose health is at risk. And would we really exchange *anything* for our health?

Would we exchange our sanity? Would you rather be healthy of body but paralyzed in mind, or healthy in mind but paralyzed in body?

The argument against health is the same as the argument against pleasure: it does not fulfill our distinctively human part, only our animal body. Health may be a means to our human end, or a secondary ingredient in it, but it cannot be the final end. If our happiness can be greater than animal happiness, but animal bodies are superior to ours in many ways, then our happiness cannot be merely bodily health.

HONOR

Honor, fame, or glory seems to be the end, because it is the thing we work for. Being known and admired by others seems like an A grade for the course of life. And millions seek it.

But again, millions can be wrong. And if it is like a grade for a course, then that is *not* the end for which you take the course, only an index or certification that you have attained the end, which is knowledge. Only when you prove your knowledge on the exam do you get your A. If you would rather have the A than the knowledge, even then the A is only sought as a means to a further end, such as a better-paying job.

The argument against honor is that you want to be honored by those who know you, not those who don't, and by the wise, not by fools. In other words, you want to *deserve* honor. But that means you must have some other quality that makes you deserve honor, like the knowledge you demonstrate to get your A. It is that other quality, whatever it is, that is your end, not honor.

Honor cannot be our greatest good and the meaning of

happiness because honor is in the minds of those who pay you honor; but happiness is in you, not in others' minds. Therefore honor and happiness cannot be identical.

POWER

Power seems to be the *summum bonum* because it is godlike; it makes us like "Almighty God."

But God is not only all-powerful but also all-good. Human power, unlike divine power, can be used for evil as well as for good. Power does not make us godlike unless it also makes us good. And it doesn't. If anything, it makes us evil: "All power tends to corrupt, and absolute power corrupts absolutely" (Lord Acton).

The argument against power is the same as the argument against money: power by its nature is a mere means, not an end—a means to get or keep or control or make or destroy or change something. But the greatest good is our end. Therefore power is not our greatest good.

PEACE

A promising-looking candidate for happiness is contentment, peace of mind. The two words, "happiness" and "contentment," seem synonymous. Peace of mind is also mental rather than physical, thus distinctively human, unlike our previous five candidates. Finally, it is also pursued as an end and not as a means.

But just because it is *an* end does not mean it is *the* end. And just because it is mental, that does not mean it is final. And "happiness" and "contentment" are *not* identical. Contentment, like pleasure, is a *result* of happiness. It is a result of having attained some end, but not the end itself. It points beyond itself: we are content *about* something, because of something. That something is our real end, and we have not yet found it.

Contentment cannot be the greatest good because, like power, it is compatible with evil. A tyrant may be content with power, or a slave with security, or a hoarder with money, or a child with mud pies. But that does not make these things the real greatest good. Contentment can even keep us from our real end, like the grass along the road that a horse stops to eat instead of going home.

ALTRUISM

Altruism, or working for others, seems to be a very promising candidate, for it is bigger than the others. All the others were selfish, self-contained. This end is as wide as humanity. Further, all religions, all moralities, and all good, sound, ordinary common sense tell us to be altruistic.

Indeed they do, but that does not make it our final end, just our instructions for traveling to it. Altruism is indeed wider than all these previous, selfish goals, but there may be even wider ends. The fact that altruism is a great good does not mean it is the *greatest* good.

Altruism couldn't be of itself the greatest good because it leaves something out: until we know what our true happiness is, how can we know what to be altruistic about? Until we find happiness, how can we share it? Once we do find it, sharing it will be part of it, and increase it. But sharing something can't be a substitute for finding that thing.

VIRTUE

Well, then, perhaps it's virtue, health of soul, character. "You can't take it with you" when you die—that's true of other ends, but not virtue, because your virtue is your very character, your personality, your *you*. Virtue seems like the beauty of a work of art: the end the artist works for. All our lives we construct the work of art that is ourselves, and our virtue is our beauty.

This is true, but it does not prove that virtue is our final end. Perhaps we sculpt this work of art which is our own character for some further end, just as an artist can create a work of art for some further end (*e.g.*, to glorify God, or to make others happy or wise).

The reason virtue cannot be the final end is this. Virtue is a matter of willing, choosing, desiring. A virtuous person is one with a good will, and a good will is one that wills good and not evil. Thus virtue is in the seeking, choosing, willing soul. But what does the soul seek? Some goal superior to it, something it does not yet have. To call virtue the end is to confuse the seeking with the thing sought. Virtue is like the clear quality of a telescope mirror: it exists to see the stars. We have not yet found the stars.

WISDOM

But isn't that precisely wisdom, "seeing the stars"? By wisdom I mean (1) *knowledge* of truth, (2) *understanding* of that knowledge, and (3) understanding how to *use* that knowledge for good (application to experience). This seems promising, for it is a distinctively human goal, and we seek it as an end in itself, not only as a means (though it is that too).

But again, the argument proves only that wisdom may be a part of our distinctly human end, not that it is the whole of it or the essence of it.

Wisdom alone is inadequate for complete happiness for two reasons. First, to know the end is not necessarily to attain it. To see the golden castle is not yet to live in it. Second, wisdom does not necessarily make you happy: look at Ecclesiastes.

GOD

Reviewing the deficiencies in the nine inadequate goods can show us the requirements for the true good. Each of the nine left out something. It was not everything, not total happiness. The greatest good must be totally good, unlimitedly good. But all creatures are limited. Therefore only the Creator can be our true good.

And once we admit this, once we turn to God, we find that all the things we sought in these earthly goods are contained in him in perfection: true pleasure, true wealth, true power, true honor, true health, true peace, true altruism, true virtue, and true wisdom. God is not an *alternative*; God is the universal good containing all true goods.

The only refutation of this would be if there *were* no such God. Here are three arguments to confirm that we have truly ended our quest and found "the pearl of great price"; three arguments for the existence of a God who is our supreme good.

THE ARGUMENT FROM DESIRE

Step One: Creatures are not born with an innate desire unless a real satisfaction for that desire exists. Every innate desire (as distinct from artificial, externally conditioned desires) corresponds to a real object that can satisfy it. Hunger corresponds to food, thirst to drink, sexual desire to sex, curiosity to knowledge, loneliness to friendship. A duck's urge to swim means there is water somewhere; a bird's urge to fly means there exists the possibility of flight. We may not *attain* the end we desire—*e.g.*, we may starve and not get the food we hunger for. But the hunger proves the food *exists* and is the thing the hunger was made for.

Step Two: But there is a hunger in us for something that cannot be found in this world. Even if we have everything in this world, everything finite, everything temporal, something in us is not satisfied. Even the richest and most powerful in this world—*especially* they—are discontent. This "divine discontent" powerfully proves that we were made for some greater goal, some real thing that is more than this world, more than finitude, more than time: something transcendent, infinite, and eternal.

Conclusion: Now what fits *that* job description? Only God.

THE ARGUMENT FROM PURPOSE

Many of us are familiar with the "First Cause" argument for the existence of God; the argument that there must be a First, uncaused Cause because if there were not, then no other, second (caused) causes could operate, since second causes operate only because they are caused by prior causes. If nothing is first, nothing could be second, or third, or thirty trillionth, or whatever we are.

There is a parallel argument for God as last end, final goal, or greatest good. The same kind of argument that proves God as alpha (first cause) proves God as omega (last end). Here it is:

If all our striving for goals and goods and ends had no absolute final end, no eternal and perfect good, then we would seek A only for B, B only for C, *et cetera* without an end. Everything would be a means to *no* final end. But if that were so and known to be so, we would just give up seeking anything. For we seek means *only* because we seek ends. If we don't want to dig a hole, we don't work with a shovel. If there were no final end, we would not be seeking the million means to it. We would not lift our little finger unless we hoped, at least unconsciously, to attain some end by this and a million other means.

To put the point of the argument in an image: if the road of life curved round in a circle, or led only to the quicksand, we would not take one step forward on it, for there would be no reason to do so. If there were no home, we would not be traveling to find it.

Thus there must be an eternal, final end for all the temporal movement, progress, striving, desiring, and hoping to make sense. "Is it better to travel hopefully than to arrive?" No, it is not. Traveling hopefully means, precisely, hoping to *arrive*.

PASCAL'S WAGER

Life without a final goal is ultimately meaningless and unlivable. The practical, lived consequence of having no greatest good is despair: nothing to live for and nothing to die for.

So even if God as the greatest good could not be proved, it is still infinitely worth the "wager" to believe and hope in God, as Pascal argued. It is worth it in this world because God alone gives our lives an adequate purpose and goal. It is worth it in the next world because "betting on God" is our only chance of winning heaven and betting against him our only chance of losing it. If there is no God, there is no "payoff" of any kind at death. If there is a God, and we have sought him, then we will find him (for he has promised that all seekers find). If there is a God and we have not sought him, we will have thrown away "the one thing needful" (Luke 10:42). Better to throw away our right eye or our right foot (Mark 9:43-48).

Part Four

Particulars: Three Morally Crucial Issues

SEVEN

Making Choices about Sex

OUR SOCIETY'S SEXUAL OBSESSION

"The Ten Commandments? Sure I know them. Let's see . . . Thou shalt not commit adultery . . . mmm, I guess I forgot the other nine."

A cartoon shows Moses on top of Mount Sinai with a clipboard, reporting to God: "Ninety percent approve the one about killing, and seventy-eight percent the one about stealing, but you'll never get the one about adultery passed—only a fifteen percent approval rate."

Nearly all the moral issues that divide traditionalists and progressives, nearly all the radical changes between ancient morality and modern morality, nearly all the "hot issues," concern sex: divorce, abortion, homosexuality, contraception, teenage pregnancy, even many political scandals.

One surprising indication of how unique our society is in its sexual thinking can be seen by comparing two wise old men in different societies: Cephalos, in Plato's *Republic* (Book 1) and Malcolm Muggeridge, in our own day. When Socrates asked Cephalos about the advantages of being old, Cephalos said that old age finally brought him relief and freedom from the sexual follies and obsessions of his youth, freedom from slavery to desires. This was a typical answer for a pre-modern. But the typically modern testimony is different: Muggeridge complains, in 1979, at the age of eighty, that old age has *not* cured sexual obsession. What has changed between Plato's time and ours to account for the strength of this obsession today?

Not the physiology of the human body, but the mind. Obsession is like hypnosis: it is mental, not physical.

Also, the change is social, not just individual. A society-wide obsession is a remarkable change, and yet we often don't even notice it. The new phenomenon is not lust—humans have always lusted, as they have always been proud, greedy, cowardly, and all the rest. But lust has fundamentally changed its origin in the modern world. Lust used to come from the flesh, from the individual's fallen natural desires; now it comes also from the world, from social conditioning.

What does that mean? It means that most modern lust comes not only from the unchanging innate desires of the body, but also from the changed standards of society. The body's drives are natural, but society's drives are artificial, man-made, invented; and then they are propagated by propaganda, especially in advertising and media entertainment. We are being manipulated.

That makes it sound like a conspiracy. I do not see a conscious conspiracy on the part of human beings. But it does look like a concerted, unified strategy, and that is a conspiracy. And if the conspiracy was not hatched on earth, there is only one other place it could have come from, and I don't mean Heaven.

My point is not to shift the blame to the Devil here, because I frankly do not think we know much about that. Perhaps the Devil is behind all temptation, ultimately, and the world and the flesh are only his instruments. But my point here is that the primary instrument of sexual temptation has changed from the flesh to the world. The flesh, after all, is essentially the same in all societies. So why is ours so much more sex-obsessed than others? The answer must lie in our society, *i.e.*, in our world.

Many societies in history have consistently preached and inconsistently practiced the virtue of self-control, self-denial, self-discipline, both in the area of sex and in general. Why has our society pretty much abandoned not only the practice but even the preaching of this virtue? It is the mind that directs preaching, therefore the answer to that question has to be found in the realm of the mind, not the body.

SEX ON OUR MIND

Freud said that "sex is first between the ears." That's true. Therefore we can't blame the body for sexual sins. The body is like a donkey. This was Francis of Assisi's image; he called his body "Brother Ass." It may be a lazy and stubborn follower, but it is a follower, not a leader. Its rider determines where it goes, and its rider is thought.

When we compare the role of sex in the mind of our society with the role of sex in the mind of other societies, we will see a clear difference. Most of our jokes, our advertising, and our entertainment, both formal (TV, movies) and informal (parties), center around sex.

If, by magic or miracle, lust stopped, then our whole society would fail. For without lust, advertising would fail. (Advertisers know that an addict has little sales resistance. That's why they buy into the sexual conspiracy.) And if advertising failed, our economy would fail (for that economy is based on greed for luxuries that is aroused by advertising). Finally, if the economy failed, our society would fail since our society is based on economics. Economic issues constitute ninety percent of any politician's campaign. Therefore, if lust failed, our society would fail.

THREE PHILOSOPHIES OF SEX

Let's look at the alternatives. There are three fundamental options, three philosophies of sex:

1. The modern obsession with sex, "the playboy philosophy" (notice it's "play*boy*," not "play*man*").

2. The ancient philosophy that ignores or demeans matter, the body, and sex (historically, this is called Gnosticism).

3. Between the two extremes, the Christian philosophy: that sex is sacred and sacramental.

Surprisingly, the modern obsession is in a way closer to Christianity than ancient Gnosticism is, for in its own perverted way the obsession pays tribute to sex's sacredness, or at least specialness. It is no accident that the obsession arose in a formerly Christian society.

The connection is not that Christianity is also obsessed with sex. Only one of the Ten Commandments (or at most two) concern sex. Jesus talked ten times more about greed than lust. Then why does it seem to non-Christians that Christians have a hangup about sex? Because an addict naturally projects his own obsession onto his critics. If a parent criticizes a teenager's marijuana addiction even once a month, the teenager will probably respond, "That's your hangup. You're always harping on it!" An adult example is Dan Maguire, the Catholic theologian who dissents from nearly every church teaching in just one area—sexual morality—and then criticizes the *church* for being obsessed with "pelvic issues"!

FEMINISM: THE NEW GNOSTICISM

Gnosticism was the philosophy in the ancient world that taught that the human body was an evil and alien container of the spirit, which was essentially good, even divine. According to Gnosticism, we are imprisoned angels, and we are all one in spirit, which is nonsexual. For Gnosticism, sex differences are not part of your real self, not innate, not God-designed.

We may think this philosophy is dead, but it is not. It is the view of most Oriental religions, which are now very popular in the West. And it is also the view of some radical feminists (though not all). This is the view which opposes a woman's "true self" to her female, womb-equipped body.

How can I call the view whose bible is entitled *Our Bodies, Ourselves* Gnostic? Because when it comes to sex, radical feminism is an attack on nature and God for making bodies "sexually stereotyped." *Our Bodies, Ourselves* is really a concealed slogan for abortion rights, not a complete philosophy of the body.

This view claims that sexual stereotypes are social, not natural, that there is no such thing as "the masculine mind" or "the feminine mind" in any universal and unchangeable way. My argument against this is a single, simple syllogism, and I have yet to find anyone who can refute it, even if they hate it. Its conclusion is that sexual differences are innate and natural rather than socially conditioned and artificial— so much so, in fact, that they permeate the soul as well as the body; that "the masculine mind" and "the feminine mind" are not social stereotypes but natural archetypes. That conclusion follows logically from two premises which no one denies.

The first premise is the psychological principle, accepted by just about every school of psychology, that is called "the psychosomatic unity." It states that soul and body (*psyche* and *soma*) are not two isolated, insulated substances or entities but two interdependent aspects of a single person. Thus any important inherent feature of either aspect will have immediate consequences in the other, as a dent on one side of a coin will be a bump on the other side, or as a change in a poem's meaning will be also a change in its wording, and vice versa. Body and mind are like the matter and form of a single work of art. They are not two independent entities, like a plane and a pilot.

The second premise is that sex is natural and innate in the body; that heredity, not environment, makes you male or female. Nature, not society, gave wombs to women and not to men.

No one with any knowlege of psychology denies the first premise. And no one with any knowledge of biology denies the second. But put the two together and you get the very conclusion radical feminists hiss at: Masculine and feminine minds, masculine and feminine souls. For if body and soul are one, and if bodies are naturally sexed, souls are too.

WHAT IS CHRISTIAN SEXUAL MORALITY?

So if we reject both modern sex-obsessed materialism and Gnostic immaterialism, what do we have left? What is the Christian alternative?

It is the *natural* alternative. The most important misunderstanding our society has about Christian morality is that it is unnatural and "repressive"; that Christians seek to impose an alien, artificial set of rules and restrictions upon a perfectly natural activity.

Where did *that* idea come from? Freud had a lot to do with it by teaching that there is always a conflict between the *id* (the innate animal drives, which he reduced to the sex drive) and the "super-ego" (the reflection in us of society's rules, which is all he saw in "conscience"). Freud begins with a true observation here—that there is indeed a conflict (but not always) between nature within and artifice without. But he wrongly assumes that conscience is a social artifice from without, not innate from within, just as the sex drive is; that moral rules are artificial and socially invented, not natural.

Christian morality disagrees, and maintains that since man is not just an animal, as Freud thinks, therefore the soul and its conscience are just as much a part of innate human nature as the body and its animal drives; that the rules of sexual morality, like all real morality, are not an invention of men but of God, not artificial rules of a game society decided to play, but natural rules of a spiritual organism, based on the inherent, built-in design and purpose of human nature.

Thus, "Thou shalt not commit adultery" in morality is like "Thou shalt not eat fatty foods" in dieting, or like "Thou shalt not mix sleeping pills and alcohol" in medicine—a natural rule, not an artificial one. Fatty foods can't make you thin, no matter how much you believe in them, no matter how sincere you are, and no matter how much you love them. A stimulant and a depressant cannot work together, no matter what you believe. Christian sexual morality, like the rest of Christian morality, is based on human nature, on the kind of thing we are and the kind of thing sex is. It is not the changeable rules of a game we designed, but the unchangeable rules of the operating manual written by the Designer of our human nature.

The fundamental rule, which the modern "sexual revolution" has overthrown and opposed in theory as well as in practice, is very simple: sex is for marriage. No adulterating sex, no sex outside of marriage either before, during, or after marriage. That is the unquestioned, uniform tradition. It is not a tradition of Christian morality alone; traditional Jewish and Muslim morality as well as most pagan morality teach the same thing. The penalties for adultery or homosexuality in many (not all) pagan societies were extremely severe—sometimes even death.

HOW TO SETTLE THE ISSUE OF SEXUAL MORALITY

Our society finds this traditional rule about sex so unrealistic that either this rule or this society is radically out of kilter. Which is it?

That question is usually settled not by looking at what sex is, but by settling a prior question not about sex but about authority. The prior question is this: Do you judge and criticize Christian tradition by the authority of our society, or vice versa?

The question of what judges what, the question of authority, is a legitimate and necessary question. But we need to do more than that. It's too easy to settle an issue just by authority; we need also to use reason. You're not going to convince a secularist about Christian morality by appealing to the authority of the Bible. For he does not accept that authority, and he *does* accept *another* authority, the authority of his peer group, or his society, and he does not even know that he is just as authoritarian as a Christian. The only hope for changing minds is: "Come now, let us reason together." Even God says that (Isaiah 1:18); can we say less? Reasoning means looking at the evidence, the facts and the reasons. That's what we should be doing here.

We have not yet looked at Christian sexual morality deeply enough. We have looked at the fundamental rule about sex for marriage, but we have not looked at the broader vision behind this rule, especially the sense of sex's sacredness. We have not looked at the high view of the human body implied by God's special creation of Adam, breathing his own Spirit into him, and making Eve out of the same, equal Adam-stuff. We have not talked about the body as the temple of the Holy Spirit. We have not looked deeply at the reason why sexual intercourse is sacred: because its work is procreation, which is an image of God's work of creation, and because what it procreates, or co-creates with God, is an immortal soul destined for eternity.

We have not yet looked at the real optimism hidden in the doctrine of the Fall, which teaches that there is a paradisiacal alternative to our present state of inner and outer conflict and unhappiness in all areas of life, sex included. We have not yet looked at the teaching of Aquinas that the pleasure of sex was far greater, not less, in the state of edenic innocence than it can be in our present fallen state. Nor have we looked at Augustine's teaching that in heaven the joy of the soul will "flow over" into the resurrected body in a "voluptuous torrent." We have also not looked at why we are so surprised at these teachings.

We have not looked at the doctrine of the resurrection of the body, with its implication that human bodies, with their sexual differentiations, are destined to be eternalized; that we are not neutered at the gates of Heaven. Thus being a man or a woman is not like being old or young, American or Syrian—something for this life only. The verse "[in Christ] there is neither male nor female" (Galatians 3:28) is one of the most frequently misinterpreted verses in the Bible. It does not teach the Gnostic turning-away from gender, but simply that men and women are equally welcomed into Christ's kingdom.

We have not yet looked at the fundamental teaching that sex has three divinely designed purposes, which God designed to be one and not separated: (1) creating children, (2) personal intimacy, and (3) pleasure. We have not explored why our society sees sex as *only* for pleasure and intimacy, with children only an extra *option*, or even an "accident." The implications of this change of fundamental vision go far beyond the morality of methods of birth control, and the latter cannot be understood without the former.

THE CATEGORY OF THE SACRED

Above all, we have not looked at the most fundamental difference of all between our society and all previous societies regarding the way we all spontaneously look at sex. I mean we have not yet explored the loss of the whole dimension or category of the sacred.

There is a very good book on this, Christopher Derrick's *Sex and Sacredness.* It is the most important book about sex that I have ever read. I often use it in courses on philosophy of human sexuality, but it never fails to produce utter consternation and incomprehension in half my students, even though it is a very well-written book. The reason is that the students just don't understand the meaning of the word "sacred." They try to understand, but they have no experience, no sensibility behind the understanding. It is like a blind man trying to understand colors.

It's often said that our society is regressing to paganism. I wish it would. That would be progress, not regress. Paganism, like Christianity, had a strong sense of the sacred. Paganism was like a virgin, Christianity is like a married person, our society is like a divorcee. When you abandon the faith, you don't just go back to being what you were before you believed, any more than a divorcee becomes a virgin. Something is lost. One of those things is the sense of the sacred.

Reason alone can no more restore this missing sense than it can restore sight to the blind. Explaining the reasons for the sacredness of sex may reinforce the beliefs of believers, but it will not convince the unbelievers. For the unbelievers are not *irrational,* they just don't *see* the meaning of the sacred because they've never had any experience of it. They reduce "the fear of God" to a craven, infantile thing, and think that early childhood religious education should consist largely in eradicating from the souls of young people that very thing which the Bible calls the beginning of wisdom (Proverbs 9:10).

They think of "the sacred" or "the holy" as a merely sociological term, describing religious institutions, buildings, books, and the like. If they use it as a psychological term (which it is), they misunderstand it and confuse it with *morality.* It is *connected* with morality in the Bible, because the same God who is the object of sacred fear and awe is also the author of the moral law. Morality and sacredness are not the same sense. The sense of the sacred is not rational, as morality is; it is a deep emotion—one that a secular society simply no longer feels. And I know no sure way to restore it. Perhaps only God can.

So the following rational explanation for the sacredness of sex will not convince secularists. But here it is anyway. Sex is sacred for three reasons, corresponding to the three divinely designed purposes of sex. First, procreation is sacred because it procreates, under God, an immortal soul. Second, sexual intimacy is sacred because it powerfully expresses God's spiritual intimacy and love with his people. That is also the reason for absolute fidelity: fidelity is a divine attribute. Third, even erotic pleasure is a sacred symbol, a natural analogy of mystical experience, the self-forgetful, self-giving that is the very life of the Trinity. It is an image in matter of the eternal ecstasy of soul that we are destined for in heaven. It is a sort of embodied out-of-the-body experience.

Is sexual morality more or less serious than the rest of morality? Without the sense of the sacred, we cannot understand the answer to this question.

The answer is: objectively, sexual sin is usually more serious because it profanes something sacred; but subjectively, it is usually less serious because only part of the will is involved. Let's look at these two points in order.

Because sex is sacred, sexual sin is a kind of blasphemy. Adultery is more like spitting on a crucifix than like robbing a bank. It is a sin in the sacred order, not just the secular. Thus it is especially serious objectively because its object is especially sacred.

But it is usually less serious subjectively than cold, calculating, controlled sins because sexual sins are usually sins of weakness, not of pride. Often the will is only partly involved, though the emotions are totally involved. It is similar to drug addiction and suicide: objectively, they do terrible harm, but the subjective guilt is lessened by the person's confused and clouded mind and weak will. Indeed that is precisely part of the great harm done by such sins: the clouding of the mind.

If the secularist does not understand the category of the sacred, he will make one of two mistakes about Christian sexual morality. He will think either that it treats sexual matters far too seriously or that it is rightfully lenient about sexual sins because at least the heart of the sinner has some kind of love, not hate. Each mistake fails to see the other half of the distinction above.

SEX AND MONEY CONFUSED

Our secular society is so far from understanding the sacredness of sex that it often tends to treat sex like money—as a medium of exchange of mere fun and convenience, not a holy thing in itself. This means two things: that sex is treated as a mere *means,* not an end, and that it is often treated as a means *of exchange,* not solely as a means of reproduction.

Our society treats money, on the other hand, as it should treat sex. Not that the true sense of the sacred, the holy and awesome, is attached to it. But something quite close to that: it is worshiped, it is treated as an end. Also, in a capitalist society the purpose of money is to reproduce itself, *i.e.,* profit, interest. Interest, or usury, as it used to be called, was condemned as unnatural by nearly all ancient Jewish, Christian, and Muslim teachers because it was thought unnatural for money to reproduce itself.

Thus we moderns treat sex like money and money like sex. First, sex is often a means of exchange while money is an end. Second, we say no to reproduction in sex (by contraception) and yes to reproduction in money (by usury). I do not say that the ethical arguments about contraception and usury are simple or obvious. But I say that there is something very strange here; and the moralists who argue for these two practices usually don't see the larger picture, don't see the strangeness of our society and the great difference between us and our predecessors.

SATANIC STRATEGY?

Who stole the sense of the sacred from us? Is it indeed a conspiracy? Without pretending to be privy to the planning sessions in hell's war room, I think we can see what the strategy is pretty clearly. It is a strategy we had better know clearly if we are to counter it, for we are in a war. We are participants, not observers.

The strategy has at least seven points to it. Let's imagine them as a set of satanic instructions to tempters, as in C.S. Lewis' famous *Screwtape Letters*, from hell's point of view.

1. The basic goal is to destroy the sense of the sacred. That will make sex manipulable by removing the old sacred taboos surrounding it. Think of a taboo as something negative rather than positive and as something silly rather than something profound.

2. Once sex is secularized, the stability of the family will decline. Weaken and then destroy sexual fidelity, chastity, and monogamy, and you will weaken and then destroy the family. This is the most practical reason for the old sexual taboos, from the point of view of our enemy (God). The family is the only place children are guaranteed security and protection from the competitive society around them, the only place "where if you go there they have to take you in." It is the only place children learn they're loved not for their performance but for themselves, not for what they can do but for what they are. Hell can influence the outside society more easily than it can influence the family, especially since the society is much more secular than families, and the opinion molders of the two most influential social institutions, education and media, are overwhelmingly secular. Once we destroy the family, we will have a whole society of uprooted urban cowboys and playboys.

3. Emphasize sexual temptations because you can get at them so easily there. That's their weak point, their soft underbelly. It's true that a soul is more securely bound for hell if it can be obsessed with pride, but it's much easier to get it obsessed with lust. Hell's ideal plan is to do both, but to start with the easier obsession. *Then* we can foster pride as the next step, by destroying the sense of guilt, getting them to rationalize their "new morality," and to feel superior to all those old moralists and prophets of the "old morality." That's the strategy and the order; first disobedience, then rationalization, then pride.

4. Not only pride but even violence can be a result of lust. The obvious example is abortion, which some of its defenders candidly call "the trump card of the sexual revolution." You see, an addict will do *anything* for his drug. It's not that lust is the most important thing, but that it leads to so many other important things.

5. Their sexual obsession will drain their psychic energy. This will prevent them from being passionate about anything else, especially wisdom, virtue, and piety. It's hard to love God much when all your love is focused on your obsession. We are destroying the old virtue of "detachment" both in practice and in preaching. Nose to our grindstone—that's how we want them, not free.

6. Freud was right: sex is not an isolated part of life but an aspect of the whole. It follows that if we break their legs sexually, so to speak, they'll be cripples in all things. People who live "alternative sexual lifestyles" will not keep their "alternative" morality isolated from other areas of their lives besides sex. Remember, an addict will do *anything* for his fix.

7. Finally, keep them spouting nonsense like "alternative sexual lifestyles," "new morality," etc.—euphemisms. Don't let them think or speak clearly. Honesty is the one thing most fatal to hell. When light meets darkness, light always wins. So above all, "dim the lights." That's another great thing about starting with lust: it dims the lights, fogs the mind.

PRACTICAL ADVICE FOR COUNTERATTACK

If we are at war (see Chapter Eleven) and if the enemy has a strategy, we must have one too. Here are some practical points for our strategy.

1. Above all, be honest, no matter how uncomfortable it may be. Never believe anything "because I can feel comfortable with that," as so many say. Even if your mind is clouded, there can be a clear part of it that knows that the rest of it is clouded, just as when you are ignorant you can still *know* you are ignorant. Call a spade a spade, and a sin a sin.

2. But don't call a non-sin a sin. Pathologically guilty consciences are as easily manipulated as pathologically shameless consciences are. Accentuate the positive, not the negative. The only thing powerful enough to conquer lust is love. Philippians 4:8 is the answer to Matthew 12:43-45.

3. Start where sex starts: between the ears. Bring your *thoughts* into captivity to Christ (2 Corinthians 10:5). Your Creator has as much right to your mind as he has to the rest of you. There is no corner of your life you can truly call your own independent realm, where you are your own and God has no rights. Not even your mind. *Especially* not your mind, the navigator of your life.

There are three reasons for offering all your thoughts to Christ. First, he owns them and deserves them because he is your designer (Colossians 1:16) and your redeemer. Second, for the sake of light, for the sake of honesty, that first absolute moral necessity. Third, for success in overcoming sin. Temptation is far easier to resist in the beginning. It is like any disease: doctors say that a disease at first is easy to cure but hard to recognize, but later, it is hard to cure but easy to recognize. Learn to recognize diseased thoughts immediately and simply dismiss them, without hangups. Remember, "sow a thought, reap an act; sow an act, reap a habit; sow a habit, reap a character; sow a character, reap a destiny."

4. There must be no hesitation and no compromise at all. The key to resisting temptation in any area of life is the word "immediately." You should have the habitual attitude that to choose sin is simply not an option, simply un-thinkable—like war for a pacifist, or biblical error for a fundamentalist, or divorce and remarriage for an orthodox Catholic. Not having these options is wonderfully freeing.

5. When you fall (even the saints do, repeatedly), just pick yourself up and start over. Brother Lawrence, in *The Practice of the Presence of God,* lives this way: "When he failed in his duty, he only confessed his fault, saying to God, 'I shall never do otherwise if You leave me to myself.'" That is what St. Paul said too in Romans 7:18. The next step is Romans 8:6-9.

To repent past sin is to be forgiven and freed from the sin and also from the past. To repent is to live in the present, the only real time there is, not in the past, which is over and dead. Every present moment is a new beginning.

6. Aquinas says that God sometimes does not give us the grace to overcome one sin because he sees that if he did, we would fall into an even worse sin, like a doctor who tolerates a lesser disease in order to cure a greater one. I think he often withholds grace to avoid some obvious sin, such as sexual sins, to keep us from the less obvious but much worse sin of pride. (Pride is the worst sin because it is impenitent, it does not repent, and therefore it will not receive the forgiveness that God always offers.) Therefore to overcome lust we must first overcome pride.

The only way I know to overcome pride is prayer. Only when you are in the presence of God do you know how tiny you really are. Humility is simply realism, living in the real world, putting yourself in real, true perspective. God's perspective is true perspective. Therefore you must put yourself in the presence of God to put yourself in true perspective.

Prayer gives you the realization of God's presence. This realization is not necessarily by feelings but by faith. The realization of God's presence gives you true perspective. True perspective gives you humility. Humility overcomes pride. Overcoming pride helps overcome lust.

Any sin is prevented by placing yourself in the presence of God, because God and sin are total opposites. We always turn our mind away from God's presence before we turn our will away from obedience to his laws. The simplest of all solutions to sin is prayer. Not hectic, desperate, worried, demanding prayer, but time-taking, presence-practicing prayer.

7. Finally, we must restore a very good thing which many of our false teachers have told us is a very bad thing: fear.

When you are on a battlefield with live bullets whistling near your head, a healthy fear is both realistic and necessary. "There are no atheists in foxholes."

There are three very good fear-related reasons for avoiding illicit sex. First, fear of death. AIDS, for example, is fatal. Second, the fear of destroying marriage and family, the fundamental building block of a good society. People who have sex before marriage are more than twice as likely to divorce when they do marry. Third, the fear of God. God is love, but God is also holy and must punish sin. God is love, but love does not force you, it leaves you free—free to say yes *or no* to God. Saying no to God is saying no to your own joy—the very joy sin seeks. Thus Augustine says, "Seek what you seek [joy], but it is not where you seek it [sin]."

Sin is like drugs: as drugs destroy brain cells, sin destroys soul cells. Unrepented sin destroys the very life of the soul. Put plainly, unrepented sin sends you to hell. I did not invent that idea. It was taught, many times, by the most tender, compassionate, forgiving Man who ever lived. His arms are the only safe place to flee to in order to defeat sin and find joy.

EIGHT

The Most Critical Moral Issue of Our Time

A BOOK ON MAKING CHOICES would be guilty of a serious omission if it neglected the most critical moral issue and moral choice of our time. Abortion is that issue because it is about two crucially important things: choice and life. Both are things people want to be "pro." No one labels themselves "anti-choice" or "anti-life," only "pro-choice" and "pro-life." Is it possible to be both pro-choice and pro-life?

Perhaps the reader is already thinking: A chapter on abortion? Ho, hum. I think I'll skip this one. I've heard all the arguments, and I'm sick of it. Why rake through that old stuff again?

Because you probably *haven't* heard all the arguments, or even the most important ones, but only what the newspapers, magazines, TV, and movies let you hear. That's not the whole story, by a long shot. Do you dare to look at the real arguments?

Why a whole chapter on abortion? Because the next American civil war may be over abortion. It's the only issue both sides are absolutely unyielding about, both sides see as a life-or-death struggle, and both sides refuse to quit on, *ever*.

On every other issue, a mediating, compromise position is possible, but not on this one.

For there are only two possibilities. Either abortion is murder, and its victims are human beings, children, *our* children; *or,* if not, then legal restrictions against abortion are an intolerable, arbitrary, tyrannical imposition on a woman's freedom. Either abortion is intolerable, or laws against it are intolerable. Neither side can honestly compromise its principles and tolerate the intolerable. For neither murder nor tyranny are tolerable.

If there is no hope of compromise without one side compromising its moral honesty, what hope is there of honestly resolving the dispute? Only one: truth, seeing the truth, education in the truth, discovering the truth. How? By rational persuasion, by intellectual conversion. *One* of the two sides *must* be very, very wrong. That is simply the logic of the issue. This side must be convinced by the other, converted to truth by reason, not by propaganda and pressure and power and politics.

There is only one way to resolve such a dispute: scrupulous honesty, passionate honesty on all sides. No one will ever persuade anyone of anything unless both are honest, and seek truth more than victory.

Honesty is a moral virtue, a matter of the will. Honesty means willing the truth with the whole of your heart.

This demands sacrifice. We have little hope of attaining honesty unless we realize how demanding it is. It demands sacrifice of self-will, self-image, the desire to win, and the comfort of being right.

The "honesty" often praised today is usually only *emotional* honesty with *others,* not *intellectual* honesty with one's *self;* only "letting it all hang out," not asking what is the real truth. Sometimes "honesty" is only a code word for shamelessness. Rarely does it mean the absolute, fanatical, selfless love of truth.

Honesty includes both objectivity and passion. The two are not opposed. An honest conviction can be held passionately, but it was arrived at objectively, *after* the honest search for truth. A dishonest conviction, or a prejudice, is one arrived at *before.*

But if you don't believe in truth, and in our ability to find it, then honesty becomes impossible. If Freud is right, all reasoning is only rationalizing, "supporting illusions with arguments." But Freud *can't* be right, because if he were, if it were true that all reasoning is mere rationalizing, then Freud's reasoning is also only rationalizing, and not the real truth. It contradicts itself: it says, in effect, it is true that there is no truth.

If we lose our old-fashioned, common-sensical belief in objective truth, as the media and educational establishments have largely done, then we will either simply cease to care about the truth (which is spiritual death), or else we will fight with weapons instead of reasons (which is physical death, if the weapons are deadly). If we no longer believe in a real right and wrong, we will no longer seek the real right so that we can make it mighty, but we will simply accept might and pin on it the label of "right."

Is there a conclusive substantive *argument* that settles the issue? Can we prove that abortion is either good enough to be legalized or bad enough to be outlawed?

The case against legalized abortion rests on four premises, or assumptions. Grant these four premises, and the conclusion inescapably and necessarily follows that abortion must be outlawed. The pro-choice advocate must deny one of the four premises of this basic pro-life argument in order to escape its pro-life conclusion. Let's see what the argument is, and then how pro-choice advocates try to escape it.

The four premises are (1) a religious premise, (2) an ethical premise, (3) a scientific premise, and (4) a legal premise.

ONE: THE RELIGIOUS PREMISE

The first, most important and most ignored premise is the religious premise. Yes, it's true: the case against abortion does rest on religious grounds, not those of any particular religion, but rather on the category of the sacred. The premise is that *every human life is sacred*. Its value is absolute, not relative—not relative to money, or convenience, or other people's desires, or society's opinions. The value of my life does not depend on whether I am convenient or inconvenient to you; on whether you desire me to live or die; or on whether my society accepts me. A German Jew had the same right to life as a German Gentile, even if the German society did not acknowledge that right.

A way to formulate this idea is simply that: Each person is an end and not a means, and should be treated as such.

This principle is true whether anyone knows it or not, agrees with it or not, practices it or not. Every person *is* in fact an end and not a means. If we treat people as means and things as ends instead of vice versa, if we love things and use people instead of using things and loving people, then we reverse reality's order. We violate reality, just as when we pretend to be a bird and jump out of a tree. We are *wrong* just as we are when we say the sky is green. The reason loving people is *good* is because it is *true*. People *are* ends, that's why we should *treat* them as ends. This is the old-fashioned notion of objective truth and objective values. The intrinsic value of a person as an end is a *fact*.

I call it a fact not because it can be *proved* in the same way scientific facts can be proved, but because it is *true* in the same way scientific facts are true: objectively, independent of our opinions, whether we know it or not.

I call this a "religious" premise because it speaks about something sacred, something of absolute value. One need not adhere to any particular religious faith to accept this; in that sense it is not a matter of faith. But it is not provable by argument either. Rather, we all have an innate power to know the sacred, just as we have an innate power to know what we ought to do ("conscience"). We all know it is simply wrong, always wrong, wrong in itself, to kill innocent human beings. We all know, deep down, the "sacredness" of human life.

Although the reality of the sacred cannot be proved from any prior premises, we can argue for it by showing the practical consequences of denying it. Societies that have nothing sacred, especially not human life, die. And before they die, they stink, like decaying bodies. Nazi Germany and late, decadent Rome are two examples. Our own pro-choice "quality of life" ethic exactly fits this pattern. Once life is cheapened—well, we all know from history the kinds of things that happen once life is cheapened.

TWO: THE ETHICAL PREMISE

The second premise is the ethical one. It states that murder (the deliberate killing of an innocent human being) is wrong.

The second premise is based on the first one. The *reason why* murder is wrong is that human life is sacred. No individual has a right to destroy this sacred thing, except perhaps in self-defense, if one's own "sacred thing" is threatened.

Premise two depends on premise one. If murder is really wrong, there must be a real right and wrong. If a human life always has absolute value, there must be absolute values.

A wholly secular ethic, an ethic without anything sacred, with no absolute values, is not an ethic at all. A purely pragmatic, utilitarian, relativistic, subjectivistic ethic is no more an ethic than "living together" is a marriage. If all values are relative, then once it becomes very desirable to kill someone, that someone's value suddenly drops, like money in a stock market crash.

THREE: THE SCIENTIFIC PREMISE

The third premise is the scientific fact that the fetus, from the moment of conception, is a genetically programmed distinct individual member of the species "human being." That is what everyone (except abortion defenders) has always meant by a human person.

A fetus does not first become a human being at viability, or birth, or later. Every change between conception and death is only a relative one, a matter of degree. Only the beginning and the end of a human life are absolute changes. Before conception, you simply did not exist. After death, you no longer exist on this earth. Your corpse will not be you. Your father's sperm was not you. But the fetus was you. We are all former fetuses. The fetus is not a mere part of the mother; if it were, pregnant mothers would have four eyes and four ears.

Since the fetus is a distinct human individual, it comes under the law: Thou shalt not murder. That tiny, undeveloped unborn baby is sacred, just as a tiny, undeveloped born baby is. In the words of the wonderful fable by Dr. Seuss, *Horton Hears a Who*, "a person's a person, no matter how small."

FOUR: THE LEGAL PREMISE

The fourth premise is legal. The prime purpose of law is to protect human rights, and among these rights is the right to life. Law must therefore protect human life.

My right to shoot my gun ends at your body. Your right to control your own body ends where my body begins. A pregnant mother's right over her own body ends where her baby's body begins. Law must protect all rights, not just some.

The conclusion from these four premises is that abortion should be outlawed just like any other form of murder.

QUESTIONING THE PRO-LIFE ARGUMENT

How do pro-choicers dispute this argument? Philosophical pro-choicers attack the first premise, the sanctity of human life. They oppose their "quality of life ethic" (relativism) to the "sanctity of life ethic" (absolutism).

This is hard to argue about. The sanctity of life cannot be *proved.* It should be *self-evident* to every morally sane person. Perhaps we can only appeal to honesty, and ask questions like: What gives you the right to kill another?

The most popular answer to the pro-life argument is to dispute the third premise, the scientific premise, even though this is the one that is the most easily provable. The evidence is plain both to science and common sense. Scientifically, genetically, each human being begins at conception. Common-sensically, a fetus is a baby. Until *Roe v. Wade,* science textbooks all taught that human life begins at conception.

People who have never seen a fetus, or even a picture of one, almost always exclaim in surprise when they first see one: "Why, that's a baby!" They had been told a simple lie: that it's only "tissue." It's been said that if wombs had windows there would be very few abortions.

This brings up the question of honesty again. Here is a profoundly disturbing question: why do pro-choice forces oppose the dissemination of information about just what a fetus is and how it develops and exactly what an abortion is? Why will no network TV ever show an actual abortion? And why do "family planning centers" not tell women about fetal pain and about post-abortion trauma?

THE STRONGEST ANTI-ABORTION ARGUMENT

Here is a four-part dilemma, or quadrilemma, that seems airtight and unanswerable.

Either the fetus is a person, or not. And either we know what it is, or not. Thus there are four and only four possibilities:

1. It is *not* a person, and we *know* that.
2. It *is* a person, and we know that.
3. It *is* a person, and we do *not* know that.
4. It is *not* a person, and we do *not* know that.

Now what is abortion in each of these four cases?

In case (1), abortion is perfectly permissible. We do no wrong if we kill what is not a person and we know it is not a person—*e.g.*, if we fry a fish. But no one has ever been able to prove with certainty that a fetus is not a person. If there exists anywhere such a proof, please tell me about it and I shall convert to pro-choice on the spot and save myself endless trouble.

In case (2), where the fetus is a person and we know that, abortion is murder. For killing a person (at least an innocent person), knowing it is a person, is murder.

In case (3), where the fetus is a person but we do not know it is, abortion is manslaughter. For it is killing an innocent person without knowing or intending the full extent of murder. It is like driving your car over a man-shaped overcoat in the street which *may* be a tramp or *may* be only an old coat. It is like shooting at a sudden movement in a bush which *may* be your fellow hunter or *may* be a deer. It is like fumigating an apartment building with a toxic chemical not knowing whether everyone is safely evacuated: you *may* be killing someone still in the building, or you *may* not.

Such actions are not only irresponsible but criminal. They show a carelessness which is morally almost as bad as murder, and our laws reflect this moral judgment in having penalties for manslaughter only a few steps less severe than those for murder.

Even in case (4), even if abortion kills what is *not* in fact a person, but the killer is *not sure* it is not a person, we have criminal negligence, as we would have in the three above cases if there happened to be no man in the coat, or the bush, or the building, but the driver, the hunter, or the fumigator did not know that and nevertheless drove, shot, or fumigated.

Such negligence is naturally, spontaneously condemned by all reasonable, moral individuals and societies as personally immoral and socially criminal. Three things abortion might be—murder, manslaughter, or criminal negligence—are things we do not debate but instinctively condemn, because we instinctively respect the right to life, our first constitutional right and our first natural right.

LOVE VERSUS POWER

In the jungle, power prevails, not justice; might, not right. A technological, antiseptic, educated, sophisticated jungle is still a jungle. A doctor kills a baby because he is bigger and stronger. A lion kills a lamb for the same reason. If that sounds unfair, consider this: suppose the baby were supplied with a scalpel, or with a poisonous saline solution, or with a suction machine that could break the doctor's bones. Suppose fetuses could fight back against abortionists. How many doctors would perform abortions if their opponents had a fair chance to fight for their lives? The poor little things certainly *try* to fight for life. Did you see the fetus squirming away from the abortionist's weapons in those ultrasound pictures, like a lamb running from a lion?

What makes the difference between victim and victor? One thing: power. Abortionists are stronger and bigger than babies. Might makes right for the abortionist. That is precisely the law of the jungle.

The very young and the very retarded are the only angels among us, the only innocents. Shall we say to them, "We will love you only if you please us, if you have a functional I.Q. of a certain level"? Or do we say, with Mother Teresa, "The more needy you are, the more helpless you are, the more you need our love and therefore the more we will love you. If you have no arms, we will make arms for you. If we cannot do that, we will be your arms."

What is that? It is simply love. That is the unprovable premise, the vulnerable, easily deniable premise. Mother Teresa says, "In destroying the child, we are destroying love." That's why she told us at Harvard that we, not India, are one of the poorest nations. A nation that kills its children is a very poor nation indeed.

But can love be enforced by law? No, but the works of love can. The cliche "you can't legislate morality" is not true. We can, and should, and do legislate morality. Morality is the basis for law and the purpose of law. Laws exist to implement love: love of the people and values our laws protect. The great battle in our society about abortion is the battle between love and power.

ADOPTION VERSUS ABORTION

"But sometimes a woman has no alternative to abortion." Wrong. Adoption is always an available alternative.

It is a very strange morality that says, "Oh, I just couldn't possibly give up my baby for adoption. It's too precious"— and then chooses to kill that "too precious" baby instead!

It is a very strange morality in which a million and a half babies a year are slaughtered while tens of thousands of people eager to adopt them face ten-year waits, ridiculously complex legal barriers, and astronomical costs.

Suppose there was a farmer whose cows gave birth to more calves than he wanted, and there was a neighboring farmer whose cows were barren and who badly wanted calves, and would willingly have paid his neighbor for them. But the first farmer burned the calves to death while his neighbor looked on with longing eyes. Is that not a strange morality? We do to babies what we do not do to cows.

There once was a rich nation that could feed the entire world with food from its farms. And that rich nation paid its farmers to destroy its food while millions of people in poor nations were starving. Is that not a strange morality?

There were two women. The first was pregnant with an unwanted child. The second was childless and eager to adopt. But the first woman paid a healer to kill her child even though the childless woman said to her, "Please do not kill your child. If you don't want her, I do. I promise to love her and care for her." Yet the first woman went ahead and aborted her baby. Is that not strange morality?

There are two terrible wastes here. There is a waste of good cattle, good food, and good babies. But there is also a waste of spirit. To quote Mother Teresa once more, "Abortion kills twice. It kills the body of the baby and the conscience of the mother."

We should not condemn the personal motives or integrity of all who abort. We must distinguish the sin and the sinner. We must hate and judge all sins but no sinners. Both aborters and justifiers of abortion are usually victims before they are victimizers: victims of propaganda, prejudice, and passion. Before they victimize their babies' bodies, someone else has already victimized their souls.

But the buck must stop somewhere, and not in convenient impersonal abstractions like "society." All of us are implicated in some way in this "silent holocaust." For, "the only thing needed for the triumph of evil is that good men do nothing."

MOLOCH

People used to worship many gods. According to the Bible, these were all false gods. But "false gods" could mean one of two things. It could mean they were mere figments of the human imagination, or it could mean that they were real spirits who falsely claimed the worship due to God alone—in other words, demons, evil spirits.

One of the most popular of these evil spirits in ancient times was called Moloch. Moloch demanded the bodies of little babies to devour. His hellish eucharist consisted of offering up the bodies of babies, or sometimes the hearts of babies, in a fiery holocaust.

Demons do not die. Moloch has come again. The abortion fight is not merely political, or even merely ethical. It is supernatural. "We war . . . against principalities and powers," not mere flesh and blood.

Our enemies are not the poor, duped humans who obtain or justify abortions. Our enemies are the forces that dupe and enslave them. Therefore, our weapons must be supernatural and not just natural. Without ignoring philosophical arguments or political activism, we must add the spiritual weapons of faith, hope, and especially self-sacrificial charity. It is suffering and even death that alone has the power to defeat death. It happened once before, on Calvary.

NINE

Telling the Truth

TWO THINGS ARE NECESSARY for us who want to fight for the restoration of truth. First, we must be convinced ourselves, and convince others, that there *is* truth, objective truth, both in general and in moral matters. Second, we must enter those areas of the battlefield where modern society has most damagingly undermined truth, and explore why these areas are so crucial to the battle for truth.

The first task can be accomplished in a relatively short space. The proof of the reality of objective truth can be summarized in a single paragraph. The second task, exploration of the four areas of modern social life where the battle is most crucial, will take up the rest of this chapter.

There must be objective truth because if there is not, then it is *true* that there is no truth. In other words, all forms of skepticism of objective truth refute themselves. "There is no truth"—is *that* true? "Truth is not objective"—is that truth objective? "Truth is not universal"—except *that* truth? "No one can know truth"—except you, I suppose? "Truth is uncertain"—is *that* uncertain? "All generalizations are false"—including that one? "You can't be dogmatic!"—you say that very dogmatically. "Don't impose your truth on me!"—but you just imposed *your* "truth" on me! "There are no absolutes"—absolutely? "Truth is only opinion"—so that's only your opinion, then. *Et cetera ad nauseam.*

Telling the truth is the opposite of lying. But there is more to be said about the morality of truth than that. Many books about morality explore the question of what circumstances justify telling some lies, if any—*e.g.,* the Dutch lying to the Nazis about where they hid the Jews during the war. I want to explore another question, one that is less familiar but more important: What has happened to truth in our society? It is important to ask when and why we should tell the truth, but it is even more important to ask how we can tell the truth if we've stopped *believing* in truth.

The distinction between lying and telling the truth presupposes that there *is* such a thing as truth—that is, objective truth. Many of our society's most "advanced" minds and most media opinion-molders have abandoned belief in objective truth as hopelessly backward, naive, and old-fashioned. It is much more likely that you believe in objective truth if you didn't go to college. Alan Bloom began his best-selling book *The Closing of the American Mind* with this arresting sentence: "If there is one thing every college teacher in America can be certain of, it is that all, or nearly all, of the students in his class will disbelieve, or think they disbelieve, in objective truth."

This is new. What is new in our society is not the *practice of* lying. Humanity has always done that. What is new is not even the more frequent practice of this vice. What is new is a loss of belief in the corresponding virtue. How can you tell the truth if you can't know it?

If we can't know objective truth, if all our reasoning is only our own rationalizing, then *all* we can do is "share our feelings." Thus the meaning of "communication" changes from "telling the truth" to "sharing our feelings." That change is more momentous than the change from truth-telling to lying, because it means we have not only left our home (truth), like the prodigal son, but we don't believe in it any more or hope to return.

On the last page of his last book (*Civilization and Its Discontents*), Freud says, "One thing only do I know for certain, and that is that man's judgments of value follow directly his wishes for happiness—that, accordingly, they are an attempt to support his illusions with arguments." In other words, all our reasoning is rationalization. The only thing Freud knows for certain is that no one can ever know the real truth for certain.

This philosophy is self-contradictory and self-refuting, of course, for if all reasoning is nothing but rationalization, *that* reasoning is also nothing but rationalization.

All skepticism is self-contradictory—for instance, "It is true that there is no truth," or "I know that I cannot know," or "I am certain that I cannot be certain," or "It is an objective truth that there is no objective truth," or "There are no universal truths—that's a universal truth," or "There are no absolute truths—and that's absolutely true."

Consciously or unconsciously, we must make a fundamental decision right at the beginning of every act of thinking: Are we believing in, hoping for, and loving truth, or not? That decision is made not just by our intellect but by our free will. The will commands the intellect. The will decides which job to give to the intellect: either to court truth, which dwells above the mind, or to serve feelings and sensations, which dwell below the mind.

Modernity has substituted ideology for truth. (See the first chapter of Henry Aiken's *The Age of Ideology* on this.) An ideology is a man-made system of ideas, a kind of mental game or work, subjective rather than objective, invented rather than discovered, like Marxism, or a political party platform. Kant's philosophy is the great turning point from truth to ideology, and I think this is one of the greatest philosophical mistakes of all time. Kant taught that no one could ever know objective truth ("things-in-themselves"), that all we could ever do was to impose our own subjective mental categories onto reality, as a baker imposes the forms of cookie cutters on unformed cookie batter. Kant thought these categories were essentially the same for everyone; that's why we can communicate. But our world, the only world we know, is like a shared dream rather than an objective reality.

Kant knew this idea was radical. That's why he called it his "Copernican Revolution in philosophy." Copernicus taught that the earth was relative to the sun, not vice versa, as nearly everyone had thought before him. Similarly, Kant taught that truth is relative to the mind, not vice versa. The knowing subject forms and determines the known object, not vice versa. The parallel with Copernicus is perfect except for one little detail: Copernicus was right and Kant was wrong.

In a post-Kantian society, slogans and propaganda function in a new way. In any society, slogans persuade people without appealing to reason, but in a post-Kantian society there is no hope of seeing through ideological slogans to the real truth, no hope of critically discriminating which slogans and emotional appeals are true and right and proper and which are not. For there is no longer any meaning to "true and right and proper" if we cannot know objective truth. The only three things such a society can do with slogans are (1) to be equally suspicious of all of them, (2) to be equally accepting of all of them, or (3) to choose to accept some and not others merely because it feels good, or you want to, or somebody told you to, not because they are true.

The scariest thing, however, is that exactly the same thing applies to morality as to slogans if morality is only subjective feelings, not objective truths. If you can't know which moral values are true, you either (1) skeptically refuse them all, (2) naively accept them all (*i.e.*, accept everything that claims to be a value), or (3) choose which to accept by mere feeling, fashion, or authority, not by reason.

If we are to mount a successful counterattack, a counter-cultural revolution to restore the ideal of truth to man's moral consciousness, we should concentrate our attack on the crucial areas of the battlefield. Four such truth-crucial areas are *images, music, language,* and *promises.*

IMAGES

Watching TV and movies is replacing reading books in our lives, and as this happens, images replace words and passivity replaces active thinking. When we read words, we have to actively create the images with our own imagination. But when we watch a movie we are more like a baby in a womb. (Indeed the comfortable, darkened theater is very like a womb.) Life has become a spectator sport, a large TV screen. Life and TV have become inverted: instead of TV being in life, life is on TV.

This is significant not only because most of the content on TV is trash—many books are trash too—but because images have acquired a new power over our minds. We are regressing to the state of mythic, pre-rational thought. Myths come from images, pictures, visions and dreams, not from reason. Reason began to replace myth in ancient Greece, and faith replaced myth in ancient Israel; but in the modern United States and the Westernized world, the human mind is turning away from these two great roots of our civilized heritage, Greek reason and biblical faith, which were synthesized in the Middle Ages, and returning to the state of mind mankind was in for millions of years before the Jews and the Greeks: thinking in images.

We can make free, active, and responsible rational and moral choices by faith or by reason, but we are passive and defenseless toward images. There is no critical censor at the door of our mind that lets some images in and not others; they all come in. There is such a censor for ideas. That censor is reason. But we have largely abandoned our old faith in reason to know objective truth, and employed the image-making factories of the media to take over reason's vacant job. In other words, we have turned ourselves from adults into children, from thinkers into picture watchers.

TV is rapidly turning people's minds into silly, passive, bland, stereotyped jelly. TV is our most influential educator and leveler, with movies next, then newspapers. Schools probably come in fourth, parents fifth (if they're lucky). And TV's power is in images, not in reason or argument. When did you *ever* hear a reasoned argument on TV? Even so-called debates are only political ping-pong, not a rational search for truth.

But there can be truth in images. Truth is bigger (but not smaller) than rational truth. Rational truth consists in the matching, or identity, between a proposition and a fact (*e.g.*, "All whales are mammals"). But there is truth in other areas too, in fact there is truth in all areas. There are true emotions, *e.g.*, grief at another's suffering. Happiness over another's suffering is a *false* emotion. So is fake grief, in a different way. There is also truth in promise-making and promise-keeping, as we shall see later in this chapter. There is also true and false language, which is not only a matter of logical correctness. To call Victoria Falls "sublime" is *truer* than calling it "attractive," and calling Hitler's holocaust a horror is *truer* than calling it "inappropriate behavior."

And there is also a truth in images. Poets and storytellers communicate truth or falsehood by their images, not just by their explicit "lessons" (if they add such lessons). The most effective lesson is always implicit in the images. The media know this. When TV consistently casts traditional religious believers as idiots or bigots, the message of the image comes across loud and clear: "traditional" equals bigoted idiot. When a horror film shows everyone's face as fascinated with gore, the message in the image is clear: that evil is more interesting than good. Good writers don't spell it out in words and let you argue with them. Their images do their work more powerfully and unarguably.

It is hard to argue about the truth and falsehood in images because the image-maker can always claim he didn't mean to imply that *all* believers are bigots, or that *all* evil is interesting. But that is surely the effect the image will have on the viewer, and the author is responsible for that.

Jesus knew well the power of images to move us morally; that's why he chose to tell parables rather than giving theology lectures. Images stick in our memory much more easily than abstract ideas. That's why we need concrete illustrations to understand and remember abstract ideas.

Images also move us immediately, while ideas and ideals have to be reasoned about and deliberately chosen. Images bypass reason and choice. Thus they have great power to influence us for good or evil. That's why it's so important to have a good imagination. This is one of the most neglected aspects of contemporary religious education.

Why is C.S. Lewis our century's most popular and powerful religious educator? Not primarily because of his clear and powerful nonfiction prose, but by the images in his fiction, especially his *Chronicles of Narnia*. Many readers of the *Chronicles* testify that they felt a love and awe toward Aslan, the great lion of Narnia who is Lewis' Christ-figure, that they couldn't feel toward the Christ of sermons and catechism classes. (This doesn't mean we don't need sermons and classes, but that we also need something else.)

I suspect that if Jesus were teaching today he would produce great movies and TV shows. His parables were really little mental movies. They were not only pictures, but moving pictures. He knew how much the mind is moved by moving pictures.

How are our minds moved by our culture's parables? The images of faith and sanctity that our TV and movie establishments pipe into our minds are either images of weakness and naivete, or images of bigotry. On TV, holiness is either hokeyness or hypocrisy. The image many Americans have of the preacher today is that of Jim Bakker or Jimmy Swaggart. Even the images of Jesus that are fed to us by most "life of Christ" movies are insipid. Few have any power to attract the uncommitted. Paul Scofield's portrayal of St. Thomas More in *A Man For All Seasons* stands out like a lone star on a dark night—a strong, real, honest, intelligent, courageous, effective saint who is also a real man. We desperately need images of sanctity like that, truth in images. One of the clearest calls from God today is for Christians to infiltrate the media, to sanctify images and image forth sanctity.

MUSIC

Music is like images: it communicates more powerfully than words. Almost no one today realizes the power of music over human souls. The ancients did. The Greeks, who had only very primitive music, were so moved by it that they universally and unquestioningly ascribed it to the gods, the Muses (from which our word "music" comes). Plato spends only two pages of his *Republic* on the economics of the ideal state, but *forty* pages on its music! He said that if that state ever comes into existence, it will decay first through decay in music. He made music the first step in education. He had his priorities straight.

Who today believes and understands the story of the ancient emperors of China who ruled hundreds of cities by music? Their kingdom was too large to supervise directly, so the emperors used to walk in disguise through the streets of each city, listening to the music the citizens sang and played. If the music was healthy, the emperor knew the people's souls were healthy, and he left the city to itself. If the music was diseased, he knew the souls were diseased, and therefore the state must be diseased too. So he sent his servants only to the unmusical cities to find and correct the social diseases.

Some historian wrote a book showing that every major

political revolution of modern times was preceded by a musical revolution. Music is the antenna of the soul, a prophecy of things to come. One wise man wrote, "Let me write the songs of a nation and I care not who writes its laws."

Alan Bloom notes, in *The Closing of the American Mind*, that his college students are remarkably bland, passionless, and "nice"; but most of them do feel passion about one and only one thing in their lives: rock music. What we feel passionate about is an index to what is our life's deepest meaning, the love of our hearts, what we yield ourselves to.

I am not implying that rock music is evil, only that it is powerful. Power can be used for either good or evil. It is probably silly to utter blanket condemnations of entire genres of music. That's been done too many times, and it's always been wrong. Augustine was even suspicious of chanting because of its great emotional power.

Fundamentalists today often condemn all rock music because many rock groups not only lead wildly immoral lives but are actually Satan-worshipers and use their music to try to win souls for Satan, an inverted evangelism. But even this fact, that rock music can be a powerful tool in doing devilish work, means that it *might* also be a powerful tool in doing good work. Musical power seems to be like nuclear power: it can be terribly destructive or terribly constructive. Many people, both in and out of the rock industry, link rock music with drugs and sex. That is like linking atom-splitting with Hiroshima and Nagasaki. It's true, but it's not necessary. Stryper uses the same genre—heavy metal—to praise Jesus as Black Sabbath uses to praise Satan. You may find it aesthetically ugly—most people over the age of thirty do—but even if this judgment is not merely your subjective reaction but a true perception of the music's inherent ugliness, still ugliness does not amount to moral evil. Nuclear power plants are ugly too, but if they give safe, clean energy, they are good.

That, of course, is a big *if*. Perhaps rock music is so

powerful and hard to control that it is dangerous—exactly as anti-nuclear people say about nuclear power. It's a judgment call, a matter for discernment. Intelligent people argue both sides of nuclear power and both sides of rock music. Some think rock music is too violent and orgiastic to be tamed—like a wild boar. (Some think exactly the same thing about nuclear power.) Others think it is like an elephant, tameable. I do not want to try to settle that debate, but rather to try to establish a premise for that debate: that music can do great good or great harm to the soul.

I said that ugly music is not *morally* bad music, just as ugly pictures (*e.g.*, a painting of Christ on the cross—is it *pretty*?) are not necessarily bad *morally*. But *is* there such a thing as morally good and bad music?

That would make no sense at all if morality were only about justice and rights and duties, as it is in most modern discussion. But if morality is about the alignment or disalignment of our whole being with the goodness of God, then anything that touches and moves our whole being is morally relevant. And music certainly does that.

Our whole being? But music is emotional, not rational or volitional. Yes, but our moral choices and our thinking are powerfully influenced by our emotions. That's why music can aid or impair morality.

In addition to influencing moral choices, emotions can be good or bad, appropriate or inappropriate to their object. There can be a kind of objective truth to feelings. Feelings are not so totally "nonjudgmental" as most people think. There is a truth to the emotions (and therefore a truth in the music that expresses and elicits these emotions). For instance, love of sheer destruction or fascination with violence are emotions, but false ones. Destruction is not *lovable*. If it is *loved*, that love is false to objective reality. Awe at God, or even at the stars, is a true emotion; awe at money is not. Boredom with gossip is a true emotion; boredom with human faces is not. Emotions can be true to their objects, true to reality. Therefore there can also be true or false music—though of course this is much harder to label than true or false ideas. Music is more obscure than ideas, but it is also often more powerful, like a volcano compared with a firefly.

Why is music so powerful, so moving, to good or to evil? Here are seven reasons.

1. Music cannot be analyzed and explained in any other categories. For instance, the "message" of music can't be translated into words or pictures, except by analogy, as colors can be analogous to sounds (scarlet is like a trumpet, blue is like a flute, etc.).

2. The meaning of music is so mysterious that *all* the philosophers have been unable to explain it. There are many satisfying and quite complete philosophies of politics, religion, education, and other areas of life, but not one for music.

3. The reason is that music is too *big*: music is not part of life, life is part of music. Music is cosmic. Its tones and rhythms are a microcosm of cosmic tones and rhythms. Great music is an echo of "the music of the spheres." There is a very old and widespread tradition that music existed before the worlds were created (see Job 38:7).

4. In fact, the tradition says that *in* music or *by* music the worlds were created. Music is creative. What language did God speak in Genesis 1? Music. Music is creative not only in a human sense but also in a divine sense. Human music reflects or echoes God's creating the universe. (Tolkien's *Silmarillion* and C.S. Lewis' *The Magician's Nephew* in *The Chronicles of Narnia* both use this tradition with great beauty and power in their creation stories.)

5. Music is language, and communication, and truth. It is not a mere ornament added to poetry, and poetry is not a mere ornament added to prose. It is the reverse: prose is fallen, frozen poetry and poetry is fallen, frozen music. Music came first, not last. God invented music, man invented

prose. The two universal languages on earth are music and silence. They are also the two primary languages of heaven.

6. Music is sacred—not simply in the sense that it can be used for religious purposes, but in the sense that music is in and of itself a sacred thing, just as sex is (see Chapter Eight). We have to secularize it *out* of its inherent sacredness rather than *adding* sacredness to it. The sacred is awesome, moving, mysterious, powerful, and more than human. Music is all of these things. At least that is how the whole world always felt about music, as they did about sex, until recently.

7. Music is even mystical. It is the most easily and universally available means for mystical experience, transformation of consciousness, ecstatic out-of-the-body experience. When you let great music have its sway over you, you sometimes are no longer conscious of yourself at all. You have *become* the music. You no longer see yourself as someone outside the music who only *hears* it. (Plotinus describes this beautifully in the *Enneads,* especially the famous treatise on Beauty.)

All this makes music a great force for good or evil. It is convertible, Christianizeable, baptizeable. It's said that Luther won Germany to his Reformation not through his theology but through his hymns. The human soul is like Germany; it can be won through the beauty of music as Romeo can be won by the beauty of Juliet.

Exactly *how* this is to be done, and what *kind* of music, and how to compose such music, are three questions that I have no clear answer to. But why should that deter us from using this power as best we can? Most of us don't understand electricity either, but that doesn't deter us from turning on the lights.

We can make two opposite mistakes about music. They are the skeptical and the dogmatic extremes. Most people are musical skeptics. They think no one can know anything about really good or bad music. "Beauty is in the eye of the beholder," they say. Nonsense. If that's true, why does Romeo look at Juliet instead of looking in a mirror, at his own eye? Why don't we accept the four-year-old's musical judgment that "Twinkle, twinkle, little star" is the greatest music in the world, if we think it's all subjective? Beethoven for you, "Twinkle" for him, and who's to say he's not more mature and profound and true than you?

Musical dogmatism is the other extreme from musical skepticism. That is rare today, except perhaps among fundamentalists. Plato fell into this extreme in the *Republic* when he tried to lay down the law about exactly which kinds of music were good or bad for each class of people in the state. There was a point behind his extremism: soldiers, for instance, become softer if they hear soft, lyrical music, and poets become harder if they hear marches, and workers work more happily singing work songs with work rhythms. But Plato tried to prescribe exactly what keys, modes, and tones were good or bad for the soul. It was a noble attempt, like the Charge of the Light Brigade, but a doomed one. Yet it was far wiser than our flaccid skepticism. It at least recognized the power of music over souls, and the fact that music could in its own way be *true*.

LANGUAGE

Language is another sacred aspect of life that has become secularized—and no one noticed! It strikes people as strange today to say that language is an inherently sacred thing; yet this was the tradition of all ancient peoples. They thought words were more than artificial, more than pragmatic, more than labels. They thought words were natural, for one thing; that although languages are man-made, *language* was not. Second, they thought of language as a sacred power, not just as a practical human tool. And third, they thought of words not as labels but as presences, incantations. Only a few poets and musicians believe and practice this philosophy of language any longer.

The connection between language and morality is hidden but strong, just as in the cause of music. It is far deeper than the obvious point that morality tells us not to lie or blaspheme, or that "gutter language" tends to encourage gutter behavior. The point is that language itself is a sacred mystery, an inherent power for good or evil like sex and music.

The deaf, dumb, and blind girl Helen Keller understood this sacredness when, in that magic moment by the well, she first discovered that words *meant* something, that the sign language for "water" meant the wet stuff that she felt coming from the well. This discovery of the power of words opened up the whole world for her.

Martin Heidegger understood this sacredness of language when he wrote, "Words and language are not wrappings for the commerce of those who write and speak. Rather, it is in words and language that things first come into being and are. It is for this reason that a misrelation to language, in the form of slogans or idle talk, must mean a misrelation to being." Elsewhere Heidegger calls language "the house of being." Meaningful reality comes to us only bathed in the light of language. Like music, language is not just a part of the world, a thing in the world; rather, the world is *in it.* It is older than the world: "In the beginning was the Word."

This probably sounds obscure, abstract, and theoretical. It *is* obscure, but it is not abstract and theoretical but very concrete and practical. It means that our use of language determines our relation to reality, how much reality we know, how deeply we know it and how truly.

Take the word "awesome." It used to refer to an object that merited the emotion of awe. But today it means anything that turns you on (in teenage slang). The deep emotion is gone partly because the word for it has become trivialized.

Take the word "parenting"—a quite new word. "Mothering" and "fathering" mean rich, fully specific things, different from each other. As Mister Rogers says on the children's TV show, "Only boys can be the daddies, only girls can be the mommies." But "parenting" mixes and homogenizes the roles that were naturally distinguished since the beginning of history. "Parenting" is sexless.

"Sexism" is another example. It suggests a confusion between two different things: (1) male chauvinism, and (2) the traditional idea that different sexual roles are natural, inherent, innate.

Euphemisms blind us to reality. Death becomes merely "passing away." Killing unborn babies becomes "terminating a pregnancy." Copulation becomes "going to bed with." Genocide becomes "population control." Sin becomes "antisocial behavior." Change the language, and you change people's perception of reality.

This could not be so if words were only convenient artificial labels. Changing the label does not change the contents of the jar. But language is more than labels; language is a choice of a way of thinking and therefore of living, of existing. Our very mode of being is determined by our language.

One obvious example of this is that if we do not have a word, we do not have the concept. Words are like cubbyholes in the Post Office of the mind. If there is no cubbyhole to hold the letter, the letter is not held there. Dictators and masters of propaganda know this principle. Orwell, in *1984*, has his totalitarian regime insure its power by revising the English language so that dangerous concepts (like "freedom") can no longer occur to minds because the words are eliminated from the language. The new language, Newspeak, has a smaller, not a larger, vocabulary than English. It is like a frontal lobotomy: part of the human mind is removed by removing its instrument. We need words, just as we need the matter in the brain's frontal lobes, as instruments with which to think. Change or destroy the instrument and you change or destroy the thinking.

Confucius realized this. That's why a first and essential principle of his for social reform in China (which lasted 2100 years) was "the restoration of true names." Hitler also understood the power of language. He won the hearts and minds of his people through his propaganda. He never would have succeeded in murdering six million Jews if he had called it "the Holocaust" instead of "the final solution." A million and a half American mothers a year would not abort their own unborn sons and daughters if they called it "killing my baby" instead of "terminating my pregnancy." How many people would commit adultery if they called it cheating on their promises instead of "alternative lifestyles" or "open mariage"? How many soldiers would pull triggers or push bomb buttons if they were called professional killers instead of "defenders of our way of life" or "freedom fighters"?

"Thou shalt not bear false witness" means more than just not lying in court. It means not compromising with falsehood in any of our language. False language does not mean only overt lies. Euphemisms at one extreme and violent crudities at the other are also usually falsehoods, alternatives to truth. But not always. There is a time when each is true. A euphemism can express respect for something private and sacred (*e.g.*, the Hebraic word for intercourse, "knowing"). Linguistic crudity was used to true effect by prophets like Amos, by John the Baptist ("generation of vipers!"), and by Christ himself against the Pharisees. He called them something much cruder than "son of a bitch"; he called them "sons of the Devil." But this was not to win laughs or social approval, or to relieve his own personal feelings; it was to shock them into doubt, repentance, and salvation. In other words, it was for truth.

The name carries a kind of truth in itself. "In the name of . . ." is a biblical formula which means much more than "under the label of . . ." It means "in the real presence and power and authority of . . ." It is like cashing a check. If I try to cash a $10,000 check in my own name, I will not get the money because I do not have that much in the bank. But if my father had that amount in his account and had authorized me to use his *name,* giving me a signed check, I could get $10,000 in his name. Well, our Father has an infinite amount in his account, and he has authorized us to draw on it in his name (see John 14:13-14; 16:23-24).

When we pray "in Jesus' name," the Father sees us not in our own name, in our own unworthiness, but in Christ's name, in his worthiness, and he gives us good things (salvation first of all) not because we deserve it and paid for it in our own name but because Christ did and we get it "in his name."

Obviously the "name" here means more than a magic formula, a mere sound like "Open, Sesame!" A parrot or a computer can say that. A name comes from the soul. Language is a soul-thing, not just a tongue-thing. It is a spiritual transaction.

Our society is remarkably insensitive to the sacredness of language. Language that would be universally regarded as shocking in the past is routine today. I refer not first of all to crudities but blasphemies. Crudities are like dirty fingernails; they are ugly but not always immoral. But even mild blasphemies are immoral. Using "Jesus" as a meaningless expletive is like using eucharistic hosts for poker chips. Yet our world routinely does it. It is partly because our society no longer reveres Christ, but also because it no longer reveres language. That's why you hear that even from some Christians today.

The second commandment, "Thou shalt not take the name of the Lord thy God in vain," is probably the most frequently disobeyed commandment today, next to the first, "Thou shalt have no other gods before Me." We are surprised that God thinks words so important, surprised that God's word tells us that we will be judged by our words, even our idle words (Matthew 12:36-37). Either the Lord is simply wrong here, or we are missing a whole dimension of importance for good or evil. And we cannot afford that in moral wartime.

PROMISES

Language has many functions. It *describes* ("The tree is green"), *asks* ("Is the tree green?"), *commands* ("Paint that tree green!"), *exclaims* ("Good grief! Green!"), and even *performs* ("I declare thee green!"). One of its most important functions is to *promise.* The modern decay in this function of language is the most disastrous of all.

Only man can bind himself by a promise. Animals, even when they have some kind of language, cannot, for they live only by their instincts and feelings, and only for the moment (as many silly people tell us to do). But man lives by his intellect and will (which animals do not have), and thus he lives not just for the moment (like animals) but also binds himself to his future by promises. Promises transcend time, transcend the passing moment. This ability to transcend time comes from the image of God in us, *i.e.*, from the soul. Because God transcends time and because we are made in his image, we too in a lesser way transcend time.

Without promises there could be no stable society. Nothing human holds together without this glue—the very glue that is becoming unglued today. I do not mean primarily between nations. Nations have always broken their promises and treaties, no more in the present than in the past. I do not think international promise-keeping has drastically declined, but individual promise-keeping cer-

tainly has, especially in marriage vows. This fits the gene
pattern: we moderns care more about social ethics and less
about individual ethics than past generations did.

The average individual never signs a treaty or takes
solemn vows as a priest, monk, or nun. But most people in
our society still make one solemn vow, far more serious than
a legal promise to pay a debt to the bank. Yet this vow, the
marriage vow, is taken more lightly than bank loans. Fewer
than ten percent of borrowers renege on their financial
promises, but half of all solemn marriage vows are broken
today.

This is awful for two reasons. The first is well known: the
disastrous consequences of divorce, especially for children.
But there is a second, less recognized reason: the decline in
our sense of honor. A man who does not keep his solemn
promises is not a man; he is a weasel. How can you trust
someone not to cheat in a lesser matter if he cheats on the
most solemn promise of his life?

Oh, there are always reasons. And they usually amount to
the same thing: "happiness." Divorce is often chosen
because you want to escape unhappiness, an unhappy
marriage, and get into a happier situation. Divorce always
seems to be the path to happiness, for at least one party. But
it does not usually fulfill its promise. The consequences of
divorce are almost always traumatic *un*happiness for at least
one person, usually two, and always for the children.

To choose divorce after promising "till death do us part"
implies the principle that I may break promises and hurt
other people, even my own family, even my own children, if
only I think it will make me happy. The sense of personal
honor of keeping one's word has gone the way of Victorian
top hats. We have become a society of Pontius Pilates. And
one of the reasons we wash our hands of our responsibilities,
as he did, is because we have first said, skeptically, "What is
truth?"—just as he did.

The place to find truth, and with it honor and fidelity, is in the source of all truth, God. Scripture describes God as *emeth*—a rich Hebrew word often translated "true" and meaning "faithful," *i.e.*, true to his word. God's promises are always true. They always *come* true in time. We may have to wait for them, like Job, but never in vain. We desperately need to be like that, like God: reliable, faithful to one's word. When we find such a reliable person in our shifting times, it is like finding a rock in the water. Without such people, society slides into an unpredictable "anything goes" chaos.

The quiet, ordinary people who are faithful to their God, their spouse, and their work are the true heroes of our day. They do more to save the world than politicians, scientists, doctors, lawyers, or soldiers (though they may also work at those jobs). You are called to be something higher and more God-like than a great politician or scientist; you are called to be faithful, to be *emeth*, to be true.

Part Five

Practice: Where the Moral Rubber Meets the Modern Road

TEN

Simplicity

I F YOU HAD TO GUESS WHAT TOPICS a book on morality would cover, you probably would never guess that simplicity would be one of them. But I am convinced that it is one of the most effective, powerful, practical, even revolutionary ideas we could ever believe and live. I predict this chapter will be the one you will remember the longest, wonder about the most, and be the most grateful for if you put it into practice.

Why does simplicity belong in a book about *morality*? Because one of the most powerful obstacles to living a moral life in our immoral world is our conformity to the world's structures of complexity, and one of the most powerful means to free us from that conformity and make moral living and character building much easier is the neglected ideal of simplicity.

A DEFINITION OF SIMPLICITY

Simplicity has nothing to do with being a simpleton. It is the state of soul Jesus called blessed when he said, "Blessed are the pure of heart, for they shall see God." Of all the promises of the eight Beatitudes, this—seeing God—is the greatest; therefore of all the eight Beatitudes this is the most blessed.

But what is it? What is purity, or simplicity?

It means oneness. Pure water has no chemicals mixed in. Pure thoughts have no evil mixed in. "X pure and simple" means *only* X.

We are not simple creatures. We are composed of two different parts; the material, visible body and the immaterial, invisible soul (spirit, mind, personality, self, psyche, ego). But we can seek and find simplicity within the spiritual part and also within the material part of our lives, and also between the two parts. That double simplicity would overcome the alienations, the oppositions that divide our lives today.

Simplicity is connected with choice. Every choice simplifies your life. Choice means saying no to one path in order to say yes to another. You can't have it all. You must sacrifice. Every choice is a sacrifice of one path for another. Every such sacrifice simplifies your life by at least fifty percent. For every path that is chosen, at least one is rejected, often more than one. The more natural it becomes to you to make moral choices, the more natural it will become to you to live simply.

But why spend pages (as I shall do) on detailed advice about how to simplify our external, material lives? Because external simplicity is very closely related to internal simplicity, to the "purity of heart" Jesus calls for. A simple lifestyle is a powerful aid to a simple heart. It aids simplicity of heart for the same reason bodily kneeling aids humility of spirit in prayer. Our spirit learns from our body.

In other words, here is the fundamental argument: If you have simplicity of life, you will probably have simplicity of spirit. If you have simplicity of spirit, you will probably be a better person. Therefore if you have simplicity of life, you will probably be a better person.

Simplicity leads to virtue because complexity leads to vice. Complexity *is not* vice, any more than power is vice. But just as power tends to corrupt, complexity tends to corrupt.

For complexity leads to complicity and to compromise. For instance, an amateur boxing exhibition is simple. But when the boxer turns professional, he needs an agent, a lawyer, and an owner who makes him part of his "stable" (*i.e.,* he is treated like a horse: ridden).

Simplicity frees you from the tentacles of the social octopus. That octopus is full of dark ink. Its natural element is the deeps, the junkyard at the bottom of the ocean. When it gets you, it sometimes strokes you and tickles you, but it also strangles you. The octopus is our modern society.

The best definition of a good society that I have ever read is Peter Maurin's: a good society is "a society in which it is easy to be good." By that standard we do not live in a good society. Our society makes it easy to be bad and hard to be good. Therefore, in order to make it easier for us to be good, we must free ourselves from the domination of our society. Simplicity does that.

I do not counsel flight but fight; not running away from the complex octopus of modern society but using the tentacles of the octopus without being used by them, swimming in and out freely. Simplicity is the oil that greases our backs and prevents the octopus from grabbing hold of us.

We have seen two reasons for simplicity already: it leads to *virtue* and to *freedom*—certainly two very desirable things.

It also leads to *joy.* The simple life is the joyful life. The complexified life is a life full of frustrations and resentments, and also full of boredom. The modern child, surrounded by thousands of dollars worth of complex toys, is bored. The peasant child, inventing a toy from a stick and a stone, is not. That is a fact, explain it as you will. And it is also easier to be moral when you have joy. Thomas Aquinas sagely says, "No man can live without joy. That is why someone deprived of true, spiritual joy naturally goes over to carnal pleasures."

Simplicity also leads to *power.* Have you ever wondered why all the technological advances which were supposed to increase "man's power over nature" seem to have made the individual much more impotent than ever before? Where are the great men, the movers of history, the heroes today? What can one man do any more in the modern world? Humanity in general has expanded its powers over nature, yes; but the real, concrete individual—you—has been cheated. They promised to make you rich and instead they made you poor

The most powerful people in history have all had simplicity: Jesus, Socrates, Buddha, Mohammed, Lao Tzu, Ghandi. Just as physical power is greater when concentrated and less when dissipated, so with spiritual power. Spiritual simplicity is like laser light: it can cut through barriers when nothing else can.

The Orient knew this power, from long experience. Hindu, Buddhist, and Taoist *theology* is deeply defective from the Christian point of view, but their *psychology* is often profound. They have remembered a secret our society has forgotten. The Chinese called it *te*, the spiritual power of simplicity, gentleness, naturalness. In India, *yoga* aimed at producing this simplicity, first in body and then in mind. Spiritual power comes from simplicity.

Simplicity also gives us *understanding.* You can appreciate both simple things, like water, and complex things, like friends, only through a simple heart. Simplicity makes us profound and deep. Simplicity is not opposed to depth. Reality is like a sphere, like a globe: the more on the surface anything is, the more spread out it is. Matter is the most dissipated. The closer to the center anything is, the deeper and more profound it is, the less spread out and the more unified it is. God is totally one. Spirit is more one than matter (the soul is not divided into limbs, organs, and tissues like the body). The deeper and profounder anything is, the more simplicity it has.

Materialism and complexity go together. To strive after material goods is to hitch your wagon to a thousand earthly stars. To strive after "the one thing needful" (see Chapter Six) is to hitch your wagon to a single heavenly star.

Matter is all around you. Spirit is your center. You are like a circle. Each area in the circle is *yours*, but not *you*; your possessions, but not your self. The self is the point at the center of the circle, the simple "I." The life of care for the soul is the simple life; the life of care about the many material goods is the life of complexity and dissipation, like matter itself. For we become like the goals we pursue.

The simple life, then, must first of all focus on spirit, mind, thought. For that is where our simplicity lies. You can't cut a soul in half as you can cut a body in half; that's why souls are immortal: because they're simple, not composed of parts that can fall apart.

All the sages knew this principle: that you must begin with thought. Buddha said, "All that we are is a result of what we have thought. It begins with our thoughts, it is carried on with thoughts, and it ends with thoughts." That is why Scripture commands Christians to "take every thought into captivity to Christ." All good and evil, all virtue and vice, all sanctity and sin begin with thought. If we straighten out our thought, we straighten out our life. If we draw the angle correctly at the beginning, in our thoughts, it will be correct all the long distance away when those lines are prolonged, in our actions. "Well begun is half done," says the Greek proverb.

None of us can attain complete simplicity externally, nor should we want to. My suggestions in this chapter are designed only to *lessen* the complexity of our lives, not to destroy it. But even if we can't totally escape the octopus without, we can and must escape the octopus within. Whether you take the particular pieces of advice in this chapter or not—*e.g.*, whether or not you put the TV set in the attic—you should be *able* to do so. If you simply *can't*, then the octopus has captured your heart and you are an addict. In that case you probably need to "go cold turkey" and free yourself by taking an axe to your slave master, destroying your drug.

You will probably find much of this chapter radical. But the stakes justify it. According to our very highest authority, our only infallible source, the simplicity of a child is not an option but a requirement for Heaven! "Unless you become like children, you shall never enter the Kingdom of Heaven" (Matthew 18:3).

Who goes to Heaven? Saints. In biblical language, all the saved are saints. So what is a saint? A saint is fundamentally one who loves God with his *whole* heart, and his neighbor as himself. Love from a simple, single pure heart—that is all God wants. Jesus said so. That's all.

Does that fact—that that's all—make sanctity easier? No, *harder*. We shrink back from this "that's all," this "only," this simplicity. *Just* love God with your whole heart. *Only* say, like Mary, one word: "*fiat*," "be it done to me according to your word." We fear that simplicity because it means trimming the fat, it means cutting out complexities, it means negating, sacrificing, saying no to anything and everything that is not God or coming from God or leading to God.

We want it all. We want God *and* ... But we can't have God and ... because there is no such thing. The only God there is, is "God only," not "God and." God is a jealous God. He himself says that, many times, in his word. He will not share our heart's love with other gods, with idols. He is our husband, and his love will not tolerate infidelity. A hard saying, especially to our age, which is spiritually as well as physically promiscuous. But if we find the saying hard, that is all the more reason to look at it again and look at ourselves in its light, for the fact that we find it hard means that we have not accepted it yet, and need to. It's precisely those parts of God's revealed word that we *don't* like or understand that we need to pay the most attention to.

I said above that simplicity began in thought more than in action. True, but it begins in the will even more basically than in the thought. It is most of all a matter of what we love, and love comes from the will. Kierkegaard defines true simplicity with true simplicity: "Purity of heart is to will one thing."

This is both very hard and very easy. Very hard because our habits of complexity block simplicity; our habits of loving many gods, many idols, make it hard to love only one. But it is also very easy because it liberates us wonderfully from fear and anxiety. We no longer need to play octopus, juggling and balancing eight gods at once with our eight octopus arms, trying to please and placate eight hard masters at once. When we are freed from the octopus without and from our own octopussing within, it feels like a snake shedding its old tattered skin: liberation!

What are some of the specific principles and practices of this liberation called simplicity? Here are six: about time, nature, smallness, poverty, silence, and independence.

ONE: TIME

This is the first principle, the key principle, and the all-embracing principle of simplicity, at least for us today who are harried, hassled, bent out of shape, folded, mutilated, and enslaved by time. We will never attain simplicity until we attain mastery over time.

We have reversed time and truth. Truth is meant to be our master. It is a kind master, a liberating master: "The truth shall make you free." But we have stopped believing in objective truth. We try to make truth our servant, not our master. We have bought into the destructive philosophy that no one can know objective truth, that all we can do is project our own subjective categories onto reality, that truth is not discovered but invented.

Time, on the other hand, which was meant to be our servant, has become our master. Our lives obey timetables, schedules. The clock is our god. Do you think that is an exaggeration? Then consider why the remark "You can't turn back the clock" is so unthinkingly accepted. It's a straight, stupid lie. You *can* turn back the clock, because the clock is merely your invention, your servant. You can do whatever you want with the clock. And if it's keeping bad time, you'd *better* turn it back. But the slogans of slavery bind us: "You can't turn back the clock."

We have exchanged time and truth, clocks and reasons. We tell truth by the clock, not by reason. Having abandoned the faith that reason can discover objective truth, we fire reason from the truth job and hire the clock instead. We ask of an idea not "Is it *true*?" but "Is it *new*?"

Liberals do this by identifying the true with the new; Conservatives do it by identifying the true with the old. Ambrose Bierce says, "A Conservative is one enamoured of existing evils; a Liberal wants to replace them with new ones."

Another proof that we are enslaved to the clock is our blind, ritual bowing to the god "progress." Whenever some technological "advance" threatens human happiness, we invoke this incantation: "Oh, well, you can't stop progress." "Progress" seems to be our name for Juggernaut, the Hindu god that trampled his worshipers to death like a runaway elephant. Between Juggernaut and Moloch (see Chapter Eight), the old gods are making a remarkable comeback in our secular society.

Whenever we see a beautiful, unspoiled landscape, we wonder how long its beauty can escape the inevitable juggernaut of "progress," how long before "progress" spills its spoil on the unspoiled. Eventually, the whole planet will be covered with the spoils of "progress." It is not so remarkable that good things are often destroyed and that unhappiness increases, but it is certainly remarkable that we are the willing agents of our own unhappiness and, even more, that we call this progress. Such language could only come from blind faith. Progress is our society's God.

How can we escape? It's very simple. We need not become Luddites and smash machines to escape enslavement to progress or clocks to escape enslavement to time. All we need to do is *take* time, *make* time. Anyone can master time whenever they want to.

When we take time or make time to do something—*e.g.,* when we slow our hectic walk so as to notice a face or a flower—we pay a price. We are late for our next appointment. But the price is almost always worth the gain. When is the last time you noticed the face of God in a flower? You *can* "stop and smell the roses." There is no method, no technique. *Just do it.*

The Greeks had two words for time, not just one. They realized that the time we make and take (*kairos*) is very different from the time that we are swept away in (*chronos*). *Chronos* was a mythic monster who ate his own children. It is the name the Greeks gave for clock time, the time measured by clocks, the time measured by impersonal, blind forces of matter moving through space. "It is now 6 P.M."—that's *chronos*. *Kairos,* on the other hand, is human time, time with a human face. *Kairos* is always time *for* something, time as measured by human purposes and goods. "It is now time for supper"—that's *kairos*. This makes it a tool of morality. We *choose* it. Whenever we "take time to" do something, that time is *kairos*. We have taken *chronos* and transformed it into *kairos*.

Who has "free time" today? Do we have more time or less time for important things like prayer than our ancestors did? Your grandmother had few time-saving devices. Perhaps she didn't even have a washing machine. Yet she had more time for her grandchildren than you do. How can that be? *What happened to time?* Why do we have *less* free time today?

That is a question I asked of philosophers, theologians, psychologists, sociologists, anthropologists, and even sane,

ordinary people for many years without getting a satis-
factory answer. It is a very simple question, one a child could
ask. Perhaps that's why most of us can't answer it.

It should be the other way round: our technology should
give us *more* free time. Our society differs from every society
in history most obviously by technology. Technology enables us to do much more efficiently what we could do only
more slowly and inefficiently before. In other words, technology *saves time.* It took a hundred years for slaves to build
an Egyptian pyramid, but we could construct one in a
month if we had to. It took eighty days for Phineas Fogg to
travel around the world, but we can do it in one. It took
Grandma all day to wash the clothes, but we can do it in two
hours. Now in light of that, *what happened to all the time we
saved?* Where did it all go?

In most ancient societies (Israel was an exception) there
was slavery. No one ever questioned the necessity of that
institution until the Industrial Revolution. If you were rich,
you got slaves to do your work for you. This bought for you
the precious gift of leisure *time.* Today we do not need slaves
because we can all afford slave-substitutes in the form of
machines. Even the poor have more "slaves" today than the
rich had in the past: fast foods, fast entertainment, fast travel,
fast life. We have a right to expect, therefore, that we all have
more of the thing that the ancients got from the work of their
slaves, namely leisure time. We should be the most leisured
civilization in history. If we stop someone on the street and
ask, "Do you have a free hour or two to converse with me
about the best things in life, about wisdom and virtue, about
truth and goodness?" we *should* expect to hear a ready yes
more than any of our ancestors could. Yet, of course, the
situation is exactly the opposite. It is much *less* likely today
than at any time in the past that anyone will have a free hour
for the most important things in life.

Now, my simple question is: why?

Here is an associated question. Why is it that our society

has devised, as the cruelest punishment it can imagine next to death itself, as the thing we give to our most desperate criminals, the very same thing that the ancient sages would have asked for as a Christmas present, a thing they treasured and sought and lovingly used? How is it that we see as the greatest of evils what our ancestors saw as the greatest of goods? I refer to *solitude*.

I found no one to answer these questions until I turned to the earliest diagnostician of the spiritual diseases of modern society, Pascal. I'm not going to tell you what Pascal's answer is because I want you to read his masterpiece, *Pensees*, for yourself and find it. The answer is brilliant, devastating, stunning, but I resist the temptation to reflect in Pascal's brilliance here so that *you* can have the happy thrill of discovering Pascal for yourself. I'll just tell you it's in the first half of the *Pensees*, a book you can read on the beach or in the bathroom.

Time used to be our friend. Now it is our enemy. Entertainment is called "killing time." You don't kill your friend. If you really want to kill time, the most effective way is suicide: that kills all of it. Killing time is slow suicide.

But we can reverse this any time we want to. All you have to do is to perform the radical, earth-changing act of "stopping and smelling the roses." Joshua made the sun stand still and time move backward for a day. You can do something similar; you can reverse the flow of modern time which is "slip-sliding away." How? Simply by *taking* time to do something that is not measured by clock time.

For instance, a Zen monk said, "Drinking a cup of green tea, I stopped the war." That sounds ridiculous, but I think it is very profound and realistic and true. You can contribute mightily to peace in the world by increasing the peace and spiritual sanity first of all in yourself; and you can do that first by realigning your soul's relation to time. Drinking tea can be a timeless moment, a deed that in its small way flows from and into eternity. We need not join mass movements to move history. History moves like families: one at a time. (For history *is* the history of a family.)

I dare you. Experiment. Slow down. Stop the flywheel. Get out from under the wheels of the juggernaut. Stop and smell the roses. Literally. Do it, don't just think about it. And do other timeless things even more important than that truly radical deed of smelling roses. Pray. Without a clock. I'll guarantee that the same thing will happen to your time if you sacrifice it to God as happened to one little boy's five loaves and two fishes, and for the same reason it happened then.

You see, God created time, and is its master. So he can multiply it and give it back to us transformed. The offering, however, must be freely made. We must first destroy something—not time but our ownership of it, in sacrificing it to him. Once we sacrifice the bread of our time to him, he breaks that bread and multiplies it and feeds our hungry souls with it.

I do not know how he does it. But I know he does. I know this not only by faith but by experience—more the experience of failure than of success. Whenever I am too busy to give God time, I find myself even busier, and unable to do half the things I had hoped. Whenever I ruthlessly tear myself away from what I like to call my "responsibilities" but are really my idols, when I put away my watch and just rest in God's presence, he somehow arranges it so that at the end of the day I've accomplished more than I had hoped.

He'll do the same for you. I promise you. I dare you to try this simple but revolutionary, life-changing, world-changing experiment. It will unleash a power of creation greater than the power for destruction unleashed by the experiments with nuclear bombs.

It revolutionizes everything because time is a universal feature of our lives. Everything we do is in time. Not even space is that universal, for only the body is in space, not the soul. But the soul too is in time. It takes time to think just as it takes time to walk. So if we revolutionize our relationship to time, we revolutionize our whole life.

Chronos is complex time, for matter is complex, and *chronos* time is determined by matter (*e.g.,* the movements of the sun and moon). *Kairos* is simple time, for it is determined by spirit, and spirit is simple, not divided into spatial parts like the body. Therefore to transform *chronos* into *kairos* is to become simple.

Here are three practical suggestions for simplifying and purifying your time. They are only examples; you must find your own.

Many people have a little land on which they could grow their own vegetables. Growing your own vegetables is delightful because it gives you the thrill of accomplishment ("See that carrot? I grew that!"), and because it gives you fresher, healthier, and more delicious food than you can buy in the supermarket. When people used to go to a dozen different little markets to buy different foods, they didn't *need* to grow their own vegetables to get really natural and fresh ones—yet, back then, many people did grow their own. Today, when everything is supermarketized, homogenized, and tasteless, there is much more reason to grow your own. Yet few do. Why? For one reason only: no time. Well, make the time. Unless you hate farming, make your little home farm a first battle in the time revolution. Answer back when *chronos* tells you: You don't have the time for that. Answer: I will make the time. I'm the master here, not you.

A second, even more abandoned delight to be learned from our forefathers is *taking walks.* It is a healthy, simple, free exercise/recreation/entertainment. If you have to have an excuse, adopt a dog just so he can take you for walks. You will begin to recapture the natural rhythms of the body. The mere act of walking is sacramental. It attunes us with the earth and the air. It is a symbol of life—the road to eternity, the quest.

And it gives us an opportunity to think. Aristotle's

disciples were called the Peripatetics, or Walkers, because they walked when they wanted to think—they found that walking helped thinking. It does. Especially when you need to work out a problem.

We walk the beaches; why not walk the neighborhoods? It might even transform some neighborhoods into human, lived-in neighborhoods again.

And think of the money you'll save by walking instead of eating, theater-going, driving, or the hundreds of other needless expenses that drain your money. You might even do your own "walk for hunger" by donating to the hungry all the money you would have spent doing some other, expensive thing instead of walking.

Here is a third suggestion regarding time: just slow down. Do what your doctor and your own common sense tell you to do: "Slow down—you'll live longer." It's true. You'll also get more done, believe it or not.

Try it for just a day, or even an hour. Take more time so that you can take more thought and care in every single thing you do. Pay attention! Stop wobbling.

Stop octopussing. Stop doing eight things at once, seven with your heart and mind while you do one with your hands. Do *only* one thing at a time, and do it well. Remember what your mother told you?—"If a thing's worth doing, it's worth doing well." Mothers are almost always right.

You say you *can't* slow down? All the more reason you must: you're addicted to speed just as surely as a drug addict.

You say you can't slow down because you have to do a hundred things and "there are only twenty-four hours in the day"? Wrong! There's something more than twenty-four hours. There's opportunities. Hours are in *chronos,* opportunities are in *kairos. Kairos* is dependent on us; we can make it go slower or faster. "Time and tide wait for no man" is not quite true. We can't slow the tides, but we can slow time.

TWO: NATURE

Like *kairos* time, nature is simple, and an aid to our simplicity. Therefore, to attain simplicity, whenever you have a choice between the natural and the artificial, go with the natural.

Mother Nature knows best. For God designed nature, but man designed everything artificial, from art to technology. Art and technology are fine, but they are not substitutes for nature. "Poems are made by fools like me, but only God can make a tree." Art is supposed to serve and aid nature. Architecture should fit the natural landscape, not create an artificial one of its own. (There is a strong movement in the last decade to return to a more natural, human-scale architecture, *e.g.*, to make large buildings look small rather than making small buildings look large.) Medicine is supposed to restore natural health and thus put itself out of business as quickly as possible. Minimalism, in medicine as in architecture, is the natural way.

Yet our whole society tends toward maximalism. The reason is this: nature always has a built-in limit—a body, or a tree, only grows so big—but the artificial and mechanical can expand indefinitely. You can't make human bodies grow much taller than six or seven feet, but you can always add another story to a skyscraper, or another engine to a train, or another million dollars to a fortune. So an artificial society will grow to monstrous size and complexity; a natural society will be small and simple.

Here are three examples of living more naturally.

Have you ever considered getting up earlier and going to bed earlier, following nature's cycle of light and darkness more closely? There may be a good reason for these cycles, not just cosmic accident. Try it for one week: get up at 5 instead of 7 and go to bed at 10 instead of 12. I think you will find the morning delightful, and accomplish things you didn't dream of. It will also aid simplicity because the things you do early in the morning are usually simple things (like walking, gardening, and praying) while the things you do late at night are usually complex things (like busywork, theater-going, and partying).

A second example of living naturally is riding a bike instead of a car. People in poorer countries throughout the world do it. But why should we do it if we don't have to, if we can afford a car?

Because it makes you happy. On a bike you get back to the natural body rhythms. It's *your* legs moving up and down, not the car's pistons. And you notice all sorts of things as you pass on a bike that you never notice from a car. A car insulates you from the world. A car makes life a spectator sport. A car makes you a tourist in your own country. But a bike makes you a part of every landscape you bike through. On a bike you are a participant, not just a spectator. You can even say hello to the people you pass!

It's also excellent exercise.

And it saves money. Calculate how much money your car, or your extra car, costs you per year, what with payments, gas, oil, repairs, inspection, taxes, fees, insurance—not to mention the mental costs, the hassles of traffic. Bike riders are almost always friendly to each other. Drivers of cars naturally tend to see each other as enemies. There are ten times more curses per car than per bike. And more serious accidents.

Try biking to work one day. If it isn't fun, don't do it again. But give it a chance.

If you can't bike, take the train or the bus rather than a car. It's simpler. You can relax, or read, or think, or pray—four revolutionary acts for a commuter!

A third example of naturalness and simplicity is to move in the opposite direction from the population flow: into the country, not into the city. Ask yourself this question: why do we almost always select simple, undeveloped, *unspoiled* places to vacation in? We choose the place we hope to be happiest in for a vacation. We show that we really know that the simple life makes us happiest when it comes to choosing vacation spots: the lake, or the mountains, or the beach. (Sand and sea is certainly simple!) Why not live by those principles all year round?

THREE: SMALL IS BEAUTIFUL

Books with great titles are not usually great books. Schumacher's *Small Is Beautiful* is an exception. The book (and its point, in its title) is not a romantic, utopian dream but totally practical and realistic. It was written by a man who discovered what works economically when he headed a large English industry. He found that the whole modern tendency to bigness does exactly the opposite of what it claims: it works toward inefficiency and waste, not efficiency. The same principle holds true in an individual life *and* in social life.

Small is not only beautiful, it's also big. Less is more. That is, less quantitatively is (usually) more qualitatively. For quantity and quality, like power and goodness, tend to be mutual enemies. Mass-produced products are usually vastly inferior to hand-made products. Products from small specialty stores are usually much better than products from large stores, such as supermarkets. The reason is obvious: it's the human factor, not the economic math. When your own hands make a product, you put yourself and your pride into it. "Small is beautiful" is the same principle as private property as opposed to socialized or communized property. You're naturally going to take better care of your own little yard than of the communal city park.

I have seen this principle dramatically at work in schools. Not all small schools are good and not all large schools are bad, but most of the best schools, at every level, from nursery schools to postgraduate universities, are small (except in laboratory sciences; you can't get a cyclotron for a physics department with only five students).

Smallness has a direct impact on moral responsibility. The more the responsibility is shared with thousands of others, the less it touches the individual. A lone student feels one hundred percent responsible in dialog with a teacher, but one in a class of one hundred feels only one percent responsible. If Ford Motor Company is involved in a scandal, its thousands of employees feel no guilt; but if a small family business has a scandal, everyone feels and shares the guilt. "The buck stops here" only if "here" is small enough to fit one buck of responsibility at a time.

It is easier to live "small is beautiful" in the country than in the city because there seems to be an inverse proportion between the size of land and the size of life. In the city, where you have little space, everything grows monstrously big—everything from the architecture to your insurance bills. In the country, there is enough space for things to be small. It's a strange paradox, but obviously true. If you have the choice between city and country (unfortunately, few do), why not live in the same place you would like to vacation in? But there are innumerable opportunities to live "small is beautiful" even in a city. You'll find them if you look.

FOUR: RICHES VS. POVERTY

The main reason people move to the city is money—better-paying jobs. The question about this choice should be more inclusive: is this a better paying *life*? "The best things in life are free"—where are these "best things" best found?

Let's make a quick check: do we know what true riches are? What the best things in life are? Make a list. Then check that it includes at least these four things: (1) God, and his love and his gift of Heaven. (2) God's world, nature. (How perfect it is! What a perfect toy for all ages water is! How close to angels the stars are!) (3) Your self: body and soul, life and health and time and powers of thought and feeling. (4) Friends and family and human love. (Would you exchange that for anything at all? Would you give up love for fortunes? kingdoms?)

If you are already rich, it is foolish to seek more riches.

Appreciating the natural riches you have simplifies your life. Working feverishly to amass artificial riches cruelly complicates your life and your time. Simplicity and riches are natural enemies.

Many pursue riches *not* out of the naive hope that money will make them happy. They know that most rich people and rich nations have much more suicide, depression, stress, and all kinds of mental ills than most poor individuals and nations. They don't love riches so much as they fear poverty. Money appears to them as a security, a defense against tomorrow.

But it is not a defense against fear. The more you have, the more you fear to lose. You can't hold back the river of fear by piling up dams; you just add the fear of the dams bursting. Suppose instead you deliberately embraced a simple life-style that pursued less money, had less money, and needed less money? People do it, and some of them are very happy. I know a number of large families (all of them in the country) where the kids wear hand-me-downs, walk (or "bum" rides) nearly everywhere, and have no expensive toys. They're not perfect, or problem free, but they are deeply happy.

But, you object, the kids will wonder why they can't have cars and VCRs like most of their friends! Yes, but kids are remarkably unfoolable. They see what is real and what is unreal, what is authentic and what is phoney. They can distinguish between true and fake happiness, just as you can. It may take them some time. Didn't it take you some time?

But, you say, you just *can't* give up that high-pressure city job and take a cut in salary? You *can't* raise a family on one salary rather than two? Why not? Has the octopus captured you that badly? Is money your drug now, something you just *can't* give up even a little bit of? You *can* only go "forward" and increase your income (at any price) but never "backward"? Many people feel this way, for a good reason: Juggernaut has no reverse gear. But suppose you got out from under juggernaut?

Do you know what would make millions of middle-class Americans happy? A depression! Before you dismiss me as insane, answer this question: Why did three movie stars on the Phil Donahue Show reminiscing about their past all wistfully agree that the early times of struggle and poverty were the best times of their lives? Phil didn't have an answer to that one. Do you? I hope so.

Small is beautiful in economics too. Less can be more. Poverty can be riches. There are two and only two ways to balance a budget: increase income or decrease expenses. Why do we always look to the first rather than the second?

Are you at least a little bit frightened by the fact that of all the things Jesus warned us against, the thing he most frequently and severely singled out, the thing he told the most parables about, was the love of money? Read through all his sayings and you'll see.

Yet money is the thing that most people pursue the most in our society, even more ubiquitously than sex. Many marriages break up over problems of sex, especially sexual infidelity, but many more break up over money problems.

Does it bother you at least a little bit that the very thing our whole social-economic system is based on—the "profit motive"—is another, nicer word for the very thing Jesus and countless other moralists and sages from Solomon through Paul and Francis of Assisi have called the root of all evil, *i.e.*, the love of money (1 Timothy 6:10)?

All that stuff in the Sermon on the Mount about living like the birds of the air and the lilies of the field did not come from some starry-eyed, mystic dreamer, but from the most realistic man who ever lived. Perhaps it would be a good idea to reread Matthew 6:24-34 with the challenging thought in mind: Do I really believe this? Or do I patronize Christ and "reinterpret" his plain words as harmless exaggerations? Which is the more foolish dare, daring to live the way the designer of our lives told us to live, however radical it may seem to the world, or daring to live the opposite way in the hope that he may be wrong and we may be right? Is *that* a hope at all?

I do not mean we should feel guilty about wealth, or that a rich Christian is a contradiction in terms. Jesus did not say "blessed are the poor in pocket" but "blessed are the poor *in spirit*," i.e., in attitude. Blessed are the detached, the trusters, the nonworriers.

They are the true realists, these simple people. For there *really* is only "one thing needful" (unless Christ is a fool); therefore the realist is one who seeks that one thing really needful, not the one who dissipates his loves and fears on millions of unneeded extras.

What could be more realistic than asking this simple question about the complexities in your life: Does this make me happier? Do I really *want* to work at two jobs and hardly ever see my kids? Do I really *want* to try to be both a mother and an office worker (usually at an unfairly smaller salary than equivalent males)? Does this new expense, for which I'm going to have to work and worry more, really make me happier, or does it plunge me more securely into the arms of the octopus?

FIVE: SILENCE

Silence is the great unknown power source, the great untapped resource. Silence is more than noise, not less. Again, "less is more." Max Picard wrote a profound and wonderful book called *The World of Silence*. It is one of those few books which is absolutely unique.

Without silence, simplicity is almost impossible. But the modern world has almost abolished silence. How important is silence? Kierkegaard wrote, "If I were a doctor and I could prescribe just one remedy for all the ills of the modern world, I would prescribe silence. For even if the word of God were proclaimed in the modern world, no one would hear it, because of the panoply of noise. Therefore, *create silence.*"

Silence is not only external; it is also, and primarily, internal. But it is hard to cultivate inner silence when the whole world dins muzak or rock music into your defenseless ears. So turn off the noise and listen to the sounds around you that you always ignore and drown out. Do it now, for five minutes.

What are the enemies of silence? Not an occasional jet plane or road repair jackhammer, but the ubiquitous radio and TV. Unplug it and put it where it belongs, in its place in the servant's quarters, not on the throne of your home and your heart.

Furthermore, TV and movies are almost totally controlled by the most aggressively secularistic, biased elite group of opinion molders in the history of mankind. Why deliberately eat their junk food? Just because it's sugar coated? Go back to real food!

Two real foods that TV is replacing are books and conversation.

Our reading habits have declined drastically. Forty years ago a writer could expect the average reader to comprehend the classics; now many readers cannot even comprehend a popular, clear writer like C.S. Lewis. In twenty-nine years of college teaching, I have seen reading ability go steadily down. A paper I would give a C to today, I would have given an F to twenty-five years ago.

Why? Because you need inner and outer *silence* to read well. Silence is the atmosphere words breathe. Not only is silence hard to find, but people don't even want it anymore. They actually prefer to read to background music, deadening the silent part of the mind that alone can penetrate more deeply than the words.

Silence is the space around words. Abolish it, and all words run together. When all words run together, all things also run together, for we understand things through words. This is exactly a picture of our world, a world in which all things are confused and run together. In such a world, moral choice is always "complex" and simplicity is a scandalous idea that elicits a sneer rather than a refutation, and is confused with "simplistic."

It is silence that enables us to make distinctions, as God did in each of the six days of creation. Making distinctions is not popular today; people think all discrimination is evil discrimination, like racism. But there is good and necessary discrimination in every choice, and silence is needed for that.

Just try throwing away your complex, expensive noise-makers and substituting simple things like reading, listening to music, and the lost art of real conversation, as you find it in the novels of Jane Austen or the dialogs of Plato. Conversation is a lost art and a lost joy. We think of conversation as something to fill up the awkward silences with, rather than something that comes out of silence; as the enemy of silence, not its friend. When did you last have a really *thoughtful*, honest conversation about anything that was important to any of the conversants? Conversation can be restored, just by willing to do it. We don't need millions of government dollars, programs, and administrators. We don't need advanced technology. All we need is love, the desire for it.

And it doesn't cost you a cent. It's one of the best things in life. One of the simple things.

Perhaps the most wide-ranging and all-encompassing way to simplify your life is to ask yourself one question about all the clutter in your life, each thing you do and each thing you have: What *good* is this?

Morality is about good (and its opposite, bad). "Good" is a very broad term. A thing doesn't have to be a moral obligation to be good. Food is good for you, but it is not a moral obligation. Our lives are much broader than moral obligations. But our lives shouldn't be broader than things that are good.

So if you want to do a spring cleaning of the cluttered attic that is your life, here is a simple way to do it: throw out everything that is not good.

But to do that, you have to know what "good" means. Here is a practical checklist of goods. If something does not fit into these three kinds of good, throw it out, because there is no other kind of good. So running down this threefold checklist is a way of applying the great, liberating truth that there are only three good reasons why anyone ever ought to do anything:

1. Because it is good in itself, intrinsically good, good as an end worthy of human pursuit. There are only three such ends: the good, the true, and the beautiful. It is worthwhile to do something just because it is the morally good thing to do, because it is right, or righteous, or holy. It is worthwhile to seek the truth just for the sake of knowing the truth. And it is worthwhile to create and enjoy beauty just because it is beauty.

2. Because it is practical, useful or necessary as a means to one of these three ends (*e.g.*, eating, or making money).

3. Because it is enjoyable, pleasurable.

Before the Industrial Revolution, people had to devote much of their time to (2), practically necessary things, like cutting wood or hand-washing clothes. Now that machines do these jobs more efficiently, we should have much more leisure to devote to (1) and (3), to ideals and to enjoyment. Yet our lives are so cluttered with pseudo-practicalities that we think less about ideals and actually enjoy our lives less than past generations did. If this is progress, I don't know what the word could mean any more.

Are you reading a certain book, or buying certain clothes, just because everybody's doing it? That's not a good reason. Are you going to meetings that accomplish nothing just because it's expected? That's not a good reason. Are you spending time doing things you once enjoyed but no longer do, just because they've become habitual? That's not a good reason. Do you have a lot of possessions you can't use and you don't enjoy? Give them away or sell them. Do you watch TV or read papers not to find truth, help people, or enjoy yourself? Then stop. Unclutter your life's attic. "Simplify, simplify." That was Thoreau's excellent advice.

SIX: DO IT YOURSELF (INDEPENDENCE)

Society is founded on the need for specialization. Not everyone can do everything equally well. Therefore the farmer pays the shoemaker to make shoes for him and the shoemaker pays the farmer to grow food for him. "Do it yourself" can hardly ever be the whole story, except for Robinson Crusoe. But it can be a much larger part of the story than it usually is, and that would accomplish two great things: it would help free you from the octopus and make you happy.

Freud (who occasionally spoke wisdom) said everyone has two needs: love and creative work. Whatever you do yourself is creative work—creative because you do it *yourself* and work because you *do* it.

How many of the things you can do yourself has to vary, of course. Not many of us can build our own house or grow most of our own food. But we can write our own stories, and dramas, and perform them. We can create our own music as well as buying and listening to others. A piano is one of the best investments a family can make. We can compose songs, paint pictures, make tree huts and rafts, design toys and games, and do hundreds of creative things for our children and ourselves that the world has largely abandoned in its mad dash into collective slavery.

Once again, if you doubt this, there is one sure test: experience. Try it. You'll like it.

Why not? There are four usual objections to such simplicity: that it is unrealistic, escapist, nostalgic, and irresponsible.

Is simplicity unrealistic?—is it utopian, dreamy idealism? Just the opposite. Experience, that most realistic standard, will show you it works. It makes you happy. It is possible. Why do you think it is impossible? Are you such a slave? Then face the fact of your self-imposed slavery and addiction and obsession and hypnosis by the octopus, and escape it simply by thinking. Think: why is a car more "realistic" or more "real" than your legs? Why is it unrealistic to live as the vast majority of the human race have lived in the vast majority of cultures and times?—*i.e.,* more simply and happily than today?

Is simplicity "escapist"? It certainly is! Who speaks the most disparagingly against escapism? Jailors. Think about that.

Is simplicity nostalgic? Yes. Is nostalgia always silly? No. When you've made a wrong calculation in math, or a wrong turn in exploring, or a wrong choice in morality, the most progressive and sane thing to do is to go back, not forward down the new, wrong path; to abandon your wrong calculations, get off the wrong road, repent your wrong deed. Remember, you *can* turn back the clock and you'd *better,* when it starts keeping bad time. And these are bad times.

Is the retreat to the simple life socially irresponsible, like a rat deserting a sinking ship? Just the opposite: the only way to save society is to save each individual, yourself first. Your example will spread, like a good infection. By drinking a cup of green tea you can stop the war.

Many of us can't live external simplicity because of inescapable responsibilities. But we all *must* live inner simplicity, detached from the external complexity, if we want to live free from the octopus. Even if we cannot have a simple life we must have a simple heart, and a simple faith. In the wise words of the old hymn, "If our faith were but more simple, we would take him at his word."

The most important reason for living the simple *life* is that it is a means to the end of the simple *heart*, which in turn is a means to the three greatest things in life: faith, hope, and love.

A simple heart can have simple faith. Here is what simple faith says. See whether you have simple faith or not. Simple faith says, "God said it and *that* settles it, and I believe it." Do you want to add something more? Is that enough for you? Do you add to that an *if*, an *and*, or a *but*? Do you "nuance" it? Or do you simply put a period at the end? Simplicity deals in periods.

A simple heart has simple hope. Here is what simple hope says. See whether you have simple hope or not. Simple hope says, "God promised it. So even if it looks like he's not delivering it, I'm waiting for it." Do you want to add something more? Or do you put nothing but a period at the end of God's promises? Simple hope deals in periods.

Most important of all is simple love, the fulfillment of the whole law. Love comes in two parts: vertical and horizontal, love of God and neighbor. Only a simple heart has simple love. Here is what simple love says: "God has commanded; I will obey." That's all. That's how Jesus defined the love of God: "If you love me, keep my commandments." Love is obedience, simple obedience, without loopholes, escape clauses, exceptions, or watering-down.

Simple love of God is the only thing that will resist

temptation. The liberating solution to all temptations is simplicity: not to *add* some new method or technique or idea but to *subtract,* to ignore everything except: "God said no, therefore I will not say yes." Or "God said yes so I will not say no." Period. Simple love deals in periods.

Love of neighbor also requires simplicity of heart. Our neighbors make many different appeals and appearances to our senses, our emotions, and our reasoning. But a human being makes only one appearance to simple love: there goes the image of God. C.S. Lewis tells of a saintly pastor who had met Hitler. Lewis asked him what Hitler looked like, and he answered, simply: "Like all men, that is, like Christ." Mother Teresa has simple love. She asks no questions, she just loves. Simple love *just* loves. Period. It's the period that's hard— the simplicity. The secret of the saints is obscure only because it's so simple: the simple secret is being simple. A saint's love does not ask about deservingness, or reward, or consequences. It does not ask anything. It *just loves.*

Like God. He's the most simpleminded of all.

Now that you have finished this chapter, you may want to read other, better things on the subject of simplicity. I suggest three:

1. Thoreau's *Walden,* especially the section "Where I Lived and What I Lived For"—probably the all-time favorite classic on the simple life.

2. Richard Foster, *Freedom of Simplicity.* The title says it well. Full of practical, spiritual suggestions.

3. John Senior, *The Restoration of Christian Culture* (Ignatius Press). Radical but right.

ELEVEN

"Fight for It": The Art of Spiritual Warfare

NONE OF THE MORAL ADVICE in this book can work today unless we fight for it. In previous ages, society helped us to live morally; today, it largely hinders us, so we *have* to fight. It is not an option.

But the idea of spiritual warfare, the idea that living a moral life is a matter of combat, has been forgotten, just when it has become most crucially necessary. The social octopus lulls us to sleep in its tentacles. This is as calamitous as falling asleep on a battlefield.

If the abandonment of moral absolutes has been the single most momentous and calamitous development in modern thought, the abandonment of the notion of spiritual warfare is next to it in importance. In fact, it is the immediate effect of the abandonment of absolutes. If there are no absolutes, fighting is not a life-or-death matter.

Warfare is, by definition, a matter of life or death, a fight to the death. Spiritual warfare is no less bloody than physical warfare, no less a life-or-death struggle, though the issue is not physical life or death but spiritual life or death, and "we are not contending against flesh and blood, but against the principalities, against the powers, against the world rulers of this present darkness, against the spiritual hosts of wickedness in the heavenly places" (Ephesians 6:12). The war against evil spirits is no less real and terrible than the war against any flesh and blood enemy. The greatest war in history was not World War II but this spiritual war, *and we're in it now.*

There is a profound philosophical division in our world between the moral modernists and moral traditionalists, between the relativists and the absolutists, between secularists and defenders of the sacred, between those who root moral law in human society and those who root it in God, between those who make moral choices as a yuppie chooses gourmet foods and those who make moral choices as a general chooses how to send his men into battle. Behind this division are two diametrically opposed visions of life: are we at peace or are we at war? If there are no moral absolutes, there is no need for spiritual warfare.

What difference does it make? The difference between sleeping and waking. When you know you are in a war, your adrenaline flows. You are passionate. You willingly make sacrifices. You don't expect or demand instant gratification of your every whim, constant comfort, security, enjoyment, and entertainment. When you hear the word "Emergency!" everything changes.

Christians see that situation as we see the sky: spread over everything. Each day's tasks become a spy mission, an assignment from our Commander. The one thing life never is in battle is the very thing it is for the modern world: boring and purposeless. When there is "a clear and present danger," life brings a great purpose and a great choice: "I call heaven and earth to witness against you this day, that I have set before you life and death, blessing and curse; therefore choose life, that you and your descendants may live" (Deuteronomy 30:19).

Scripture is very clear about this. The idea of spiritual warfare is its pervasive, overall theme, from the Fall through the Last Judgment. The idea is sometimes explicit (as in the above sermon from Moses), but always at least implicit, in the background, assumed. The whole reason for the most important event in human history, the Incarnation, was spiritual warfare: God's invasion of enemy-occupied territory to redeem his children from captivity to the forces of evil. Christmas was God's D-day.

But the modern world, even modern Christianity, is amazingly silent about this all-pervasive biblical theme. Most of the church seems to be sliding into the world's way of thinking, just as ancient Israel did, needing but not heeding the unfashionable words of the prophets, such as Jeremiah's lament against the popular religious teachers of his day: "They have healed the wound of / my people lightly, / saying, 'Peace, / peace' when there is no peace" (Jeremiah 6:14). Peace is indeed one of the gifts of the Spirit promised by Christ; but that peace means peace with God, self, and neighbor, not with the world, the flesh, and the devil.

There are in fact three aspects of the fundamental notion of spiritual warfare. All three are in danger of disappearing and in desperate need of recapturing. First, there is the reality of spiritual warfare, the vision of life as a spiritual battle. Second, there is the reality of our spiritual enemies, of "principalities and powers" beyond flesh and blood. Third, there is the reality of spiritual evil, or sin. In the context of the first two ideas, sin means treason, betrayal, working for the enemy.

First, the Christian life as spiritual warfare. Traditionally, this life consisted of two parts: the positive and the negative. The positive part included prayer and works of charity. The negative included repentance, fasting, and "mortification." Mortification? Not only the practice but the very word has disappeared from our vocabulary, unless we are antiquarians. "Mortification" means killing, putting to death. That is the business of a soldier, to speak plainly and honestly: to kill. The human race instinctively knows that the business of spiritual killing is terribly important; that's why pagan religions are full of sacrifice, and why the most popular goddess in Hindu lands is Kali, and the most popular god is Shiva. Both are killers, destroyers—of evil.

But "the power of positive thinking" has blinded us to the power of *negative* thinking. There is a need for negative thinking *if* there are real enemies to think negatively, *i.e.,* truly, about. More important, there is a need for negative *acting*, for what the medievals called *agere contra*, acting contrarily, *not* to "go with the flow." If we live in a world whose flow goes to Hell, it is absolutely imperative that we do *not* go with the flow but against it. If there is real poison, we are fools to treat it like food. If there is cancer in the soul, we are fools to nourish it like healthy tissue. If there are barbarians at the gates, we are fools to open up and pretend they are citizens.

The cult of unthinking "openness" and equally unthinking rejection of all "discrimination" has blinded us here. Should we be open to the forces of life and of death alike? Should our minds be open to falsehood equally with truth? Should we fear discriminating against ideas as well as against persons? Having an open mind is like having an open mouth, Chesterton says: it is not an end but a means to an end. The end is closing the mouth (and the mind) on something solid.

One deep cause of the disappearance of discrimination, the orgy of openness, and the modern world's spiritual war against the idea of spiritual war, has been the hatred of hatred. If there is one thing preachers and teachers tell us today it is that we should love. They've got that part of the message right, anyway. (At least love of neighbor; we don't hear too much about love of God.) What they *mean* by "love" usually sounds pretty weak and wimpy, but at least this proposition is true: we must love our neighbors, *all* our neighbors. And since hate is opposite to love, we must not hate our neighbors, *any* of them. Very true. But does that mean there is no place for hate in the Christian life?

Indeed there is a place for hate in the Christian life! If we become incapable of hate, we become also incapable of real love. Both hate and love come from will, passion, energy. Watering the will down to a soup is the coward's way to eliminate hate. This is the popular modern way: compassion without passion. The way of the saints is the opposite: to make compassion a passion, to love with more passion, not less, than hate; to turn the very passion of hate toward its proper objects: toward the real enemies of love. In other words, to "fight the good fight." All the saints were fanatics because all the saints were great lovers and all great lovers are fanatics. Fanatics about love, not about ideology or hangups or personal programs, but fanatics nevertheless.

There is a striking and memorable passage in C.S. Lewis' novel *Perelandra* in which Ransom, the ordinary-man hero, has to try to kill Weston, "the Un-man," who is so wholly demon-possessed that he is not a man at all any more. Ransom has to do this because it is a direct command from Maleldil (God). Ransom feels a surprising joy and freedom at finding for the first time in his life a lawful object to hate—in fact, a lawful *concrete* object to hate, an experience probably no one in this world can ever have. Ransom finds what hate is made for, like a child with a knife who finds wood.

Is this hate unholy, unsaintly? Just the opposite. Saints may have more love and compassion for sinners but they have no compassion for sin. They love Hitler but hate his holocaust. They love and try to save the Satan-worshiper, but not Satan. For Satan is unredeemable. No one redeemable is our enemy, no one still in time, that can repent, no flesh and blood. But "we contend not against flesh and blood but . . . against the spiritual hosts of wickedness in the heavenly places." That may be unfashionable to the mind of modern man, but it is the message from the mind of God.

Isn't it right for us to be angry at having to drive as

hostage to drunk drivers who may well cripple our passengers for life because their lawyer got them off the last time they slammed into some innocent victim? Is it wrong to be angry at having to send our children to schools that assume people are apes in anthropology class, rabbits in sex education class, and insects devouring their own children in school-based health-and-abortion-referral clinics? Is there no place left for righteous indignation? If not, then there is no place left for righteousness.

Spiritual warfare presupposes spiritual enemies. Are there really spiritual enemies? Are evil spirits real or only myths?

The vision of the cosmos common to nearly every society before the modern West included an invisible realm full of spirits, both good and evil. The modern horizon has shrunk to the bounds of the visible. We no longer see this larger world surrounding us. Of course it never was seen with the physical eyes (or hardly ever), but we used to have other eyes, spiritual eyes. Today these other eyes have deteriorated, so much that most people don't even know they have them.

We need to have our eyes opened like the servant of Elisha, "the man of God":

When the servant of the man of God rose early in the morning and went out, behold, an army with horses and chariots was round about the city. And the servant said, "Alas, my master! What shall we do?" He [Elisha] said, "Fear not, for those who are with us are more than those who are with them." Then Elisha prayed, and said, "O Lord, I pray thee, open his eyes that he may see." So the Lord opened the eyes of the young man, and he saw; and behold, the mountain was full of horses and chariots of fire round about Elisha. (2 Kings 6:15-17)

The fiery horses and chariots are the angel army of the Lord. *That's* whose side we're fighting on, and we'd better know it, simply because it's true, it's *there.* God didn't put a vision *into* Elisha's servant's eyes, he simply opened his eyes to see what was there. May he do the same to us.

We have not only one enemy but three. Traditionally, three spiritual enemies, three obstacles to our good and our joy were distinguished: the world, the flesh, and the Devil.

"The world" does not mean the material planet. God created that, and pronounced it good (Genesis 1). The word for the material planet in Greek is *ge,* or *gaia.* The Greek word translated "world" in the New Testament is usually *aion,* from which we get the English word "eon." It's a time-word, not a space-word. It means the world-system or evil-empire of Satan, the kingdom of evil, the evil era or age or order of things that began not with the creation but with the Fall. It began recently: not 15-20 billion years ago, when God big-banged the universe into existence, but much later, when our remote ancestors rebelled against God and ate the forbidden fruit. "The world" is "the fallen world," the world of the Fall, not of the creation.

"The flesh" (Greek, *sarx, sakra*) does not mean the skin, or the body, or sex. All *that* is also made by God and declared good (Genesis 2:7; 1:27-28, 31). "The flesh" is not the body as such but the addictive, selfish bodily desires of fallen man: not sex but lust, not money but greed, not self but selfishness.

When St. Paul contrasts "the works of the flesh" with "the works of the Spirit" in Galatians 5, it is not a contrast between the physical and the nonphysical but between the state of fallenness and the state of salvation. "The works of the flesh" include not only licentiousness, fornication, and drunkenness but also anger, envy, idolatry, and sorcery.

"The Devil" means . . . well, the Devil. We can forget the red tights, horns, hoofs, and pitchforks, none of which ever appear in Scripture. But we can't forget the real being, the fallen angel, the evil spirit. He has a mind and a will, a personality. Scripture gives him a name: "Satan," which means "the accuser," the prosecuting attorney. He is *our* prosecuting attorney, not God's. God cannot be a defendant in any court case (as Job found out). God has no opposite and no rival, though Satan lives the lie that he is God's rival and would like us to believe it. No, Satan's rival and opposite is not God but Michael, leader of the army of archangels (ruler-angels). Michael's very name gives the lie to Satan: "Michael" means "Who is like God?"

Our three enemies come from three directions. "The world" is evil-beneath-us, or evil-around-us, "the flesh" is evil-within-us; and "the Devil" is evil-above-us, "wickedness in heavenly places." "The world" is our evil objective physical environment, "the flesh" is our evil subjective, inner environment, "the Devil" is our evil objective spiritual environment. "The world" is the false cosmos, "the flesh" is the false self, and "the Devil" is the false god. All three are living lies.

Since evil can come from within (flesh) or without, and if from without, from above (Devil) or below (world), we need discernment. Fighting one enemy with weapons fit for another is folly—like attacking a ship with a sword or a sword with a ship. Our strategy against our three enemies must be three different strategies. We need to disdain the world, be detached from the world, even ignore the world (*e.g.*, fashionable media lies). We need to master and control the flesh, to tame it and ride it like a wild horse (see 1 Corinthians 9:27). And we need to be freed from the Devil; only God can conquer him.

We dare not confuse or interchange these three strategies. For instance, if we try to conquer the world instead of being detached from it, we take it too seriously and selfishly. Christ has conquered the world already (John 16:33), not by power but by suffering. Or if we think of our temptations of the flesh as coming straight from the Devil, we give them too much importance and become obsessed with them—just what he wants. Or if we think the Devil's work comes only from the world, from man, from society, we underestimate him and think we can defeat him with social revolutions. As C.S. Lewis said in *The Screwtape Letters,* Satan is equally pleased by too much attention or too little, by our old obsessions with him or our new ignoring of him.

For, remember, we are at war. What an advantage an army would have if the opposing army vastly overestimated *or* underestimated its power! It is as essential for us to identify our spiritual enemies and assess their real power, as for an army to identify and assess its physical enemies and their resources, and to use the necessary weapons against each one, to use "the whole armor of God" (Ephesians 6:11).

Of the three ideas of spiritual warfare, spiritual enemies and spiritual evil (sin), the third is not quite as totally scorned today as the other two (in fact, some see the idea of sin as making a real comeback); but it is certainly still a very unpopular idea.

Is sin outdated? Just the opposite. Malcolm Muggeridge says that sin is the only Christian dogma that can be proved just by reading the daily newspapers.

Is the *idea* of sin outdated? How can an idea be outdated if the reality it denotes isn't? Besides, how can ideas become outdated? Are they things like fashions? How can truth be told with the clock or the calendar? How can time alter truth as it alters matter?

But haven't psychologists and sociologists and anthropologists explained away sin as merely maladjustment, or ignorance and bad education, or misprogramming, or genetic defects? Didn't Freud show that there is no sin, only inadequate adjustment between *id* and superego, individual and society? Didn't Skinner show that there is no sin, only inefficient social conditioning, inadequate behavior modification?

In a word, *no.* No one has ever shown these things, proved these "onlys," these reductionisms. No more than a dying cancer patient can explain away his disease as "only" cells.

No more than a murder is "only" a bullet wound. No more than a book is "only" syllables. That's not what it *is*, only what it's *made of*; only its matter, not its form.

Why does the modern mind misunderstand sin? Because sin is a word that presupposes two things that the modern world disbelieves in: a divine will giving moral laws, and a human soul receiving them. Sin means a mis-relationship between these two wills, a violation of the marriage covenant between God and the soul. But the modern world's God is not a person but an ideal, not a lawgiver with a will but a vague force with a senile smile; and the human soul, as God's image, is almost as vague and wispy. When God seems weak, so does his image.

"Evil" is a broader term than "sin." Evil does not have explicit reference to the God-relationship. Yet even evil is misunderstood by the modern mind, in at least five ways.

First, the Dracula misunderstanding: that evil is like Dracula, a great myth, a fascinating fiction, an imaginative exaggeration.

Second, the Hitler misunderstanding: that the only evil is cruelty (and thus the only good is kindness, or compassion). This notion is so pervasive that many readers will probably wonder what I could possibly be talking about here. They think there aren't ten commandments, only one. If they haven't killed anybody lately, they think they're saints.

Third, the Jungian (and Hindu and Buddhist) misunderstanding: that evil is only "the dark side" of good, that good and evil are not really, ultimately distinct but one. This is utter blasphemy, of course, confusing God and Satan, but it is usually camouflaged under nice euphemisms such as "accepting" your "shadow," or "enlightenment" that "transcends" categories (good and evil) that are "only human."

Fourth, the Platonic and Liberal misunderstanding: that man is by nature good and wise and unfallen, that evil is only ignorance and therefore is curable by right education.

Fifth, the Zoroastrian misunderstanding: that evil is a *thing*, an entity, even an absolute, a second God. (Zoroaster was the sixth-century Persian prophet who founded the religion that goes by his name and teaches this ultimate dualism. It comes from our concrete imagination: we tend to imagine evil as some *thing*, like a dark cloud, and good as a bright one.)

The first four of these popular misunderstandings fail to take evil seriously enough; the fifth (dualism) takes it too seriously. The latter mistake was made mostly in the past, the first four in the present. If the late Middle Ages feared evil too much (thus the extreme penances, the legalism and guilt, and the paranoia of the Inquisition and the witch hunts), we moderns fear it too little. If they thought of life as a hot seat, we think of life as a hot tub. The enemy is equally pleased with either error.

The inquisitors and witch-hunters practiced spiritual warfare without ethics. We practice ethics without spiritual warfare. Spiritual warfare without ethics is like might without right. Ethics without spiritual warfare is like right without might.

Spiritual warfare without ethics believes that "winning isn't the most important thing; it's the *only* thing." The inquisitors practiced the pragmatic philosophy that the end (defeating Satan) justifies the means (torture, terror, etc.). Thomas More refutes this, in *A Man For All Seasons*, when he says he would give even the Devil the rights of law, for if you cut down all the laws, when the Devil comes for you, where will you hide then?

Spiritual warfare without ethics is not even real spiritual warfare, because it plays into the hands of the enemy, it capitulates to immorality. But ethics without spiritual warfare is no better; it's not even real ethics, because the whole reason for ethics is spiritual warfare. Our practical need for moral maps comes from our battlefield situation. We need to know the lay of the land because we are fighting on it.

So in waging spiritual warfare we must avoid both the ancient, "hard" mistake and the modern, "soft" mistake. We must not have hard hearts or soft heads. We must not hate sinners or love sins. We must not be either wolves or wimps.

Our ancestors were better than we are at the "hard" virtues, like courage and chastity. We are better at the "soft" virtues, like kindness and philanthropy. But you can no more specialize in virtue than in anatomical organs. The virtues are like organs in a body: interdependent. Compassion without courage ceases under pressure, and compassion without justice is wasted. Justice without mercy becomes cruelty, and chastity without charity becomes coldness. The "hard" virtues are like the bones in a body, and the "soft" virtues like tissues. Bones without tissues are a skeleton, and tissues without bones are a jellyfish. In reacting against our ancestors whose morality sometimes resembled a skeleton, we have embraced a morality that sometimes resembles a jellyfish.

How can we learn to fight without hating, to hate sins but not sinners, to love sinners without loving sins? Only one ever did it perfectly. The only way we can do it is his way. He *is* "the way, the truth, and the life." If he only *taught* the way, we could learn it from others. But if he *is* the way, we can learn it and live it only in him.

TWELVE

How to Know God's Will: The Art of Discernment

C HAPTERS ELEVEN AND TWELVE must go together, for we need both a strong will *and* a strong mind for the moral life. We need both to "fight the good fight" of spiritual warfare (Chapter Eleven) *and* to understand our Commander's orders, to discern God's will (Chapter Twelve). It will do us no good, and much harm, to fight with passion if we don't know what to fight for and what to fight against. This chapter explores the practical question *how* we can be sure our goals correspond with God's, how we know good and evil.

There are two very different situations in which the question of discernment arises: in life and in philosophical discussion. In life it arises from real need and with real passion, but not in philosophical discussions. That is why people often get real answers to this question in life, but hardly ever in philosophical discussions.

If a student asks me, as a philosophy professor, "How can I be sure what is right and wrong?" I answer: "Do you want to know how *we* can be sure or how *you* can be sure? Do you really want to know? Because if you do, then you can. But if you only want to argue to impress other people, or to justify a convenient moral skepticism, then you *won't* really know what is really right and wrong."

MORAL SKEPTICISM VS. MORAL KNOWLEDGE

Moral skepticism is surely the prevailing philosophy in the modern world, at least in academia and the media, our two great opinion-molding institutions. They are the two most influential teaching establishments in our culture—which means that this prevailing philosophy of moral skepticism will more and more prevail in our culture as these two teaching establishments come to have more and more influence in the future and keep turning out teachers in their own skeptical image. Unless we overcome moral skepticism, we will never have a moral society, and unless you overcome it as an individual, you will not be able to make moral choices and lead a moral life.

The opposite of skepticism is knowing. Skepticism says: I *cannot* know. Knowledge says: I *do* know, therefore I *can* know.

There are two kinds of moral knowledge we need: knowledge of principles and knowledge of practice, of applications. We dealt with knowledge of moral principles in Chapters Three and Four. Now we need to deal with the other kind of moral knowledge, called discernment: practical moral wisdom in decision-making, in applying principles to practice.

We seek two qualities in this moral knowledge: objective accuracy and subjective assurance. The word "certainty" is often used for both, but we must distinguish these two things or else we will settle for only one and think we also have the other. Perhaps we should call them by two different names, "certainty" (objective) and "certitude" (subjective).

A surgeon needs both. If his objective medical knowledge is uncertain, he may botch the operation, no matter how much confidence (subjective certitude) he feels. And if his hands shake with doubt, he will also botch the operation, no matter how objectively certain his medical knowledge is. Life is like surgery. We are performing operations on life all the time. We need to overcome skepticism because we are surgeons. Skepticism may be arguable in the classroom but it is not viable in the operating room.

We need certitude as well as certainty. Wars are often decided by the certitude and assurance of one's cause. Assurance is like "the will to live": it confounds predictions and performs near-miraculous feats. It is probably the main reason why colonial America defeated imperial England and why decadent America lost to fanatical North Vietnam.

CONSCIENCE—FEELING OR THINKING?

The word "conscience" is usually used for the power in us that gives us this moral knowledge. The ancients thought of conscience more as a *knowing*. Moderns think of it more as a *feeling*. Which is it? Does it give certitude in feeling or certainty in knowledge?

Both. But if our conscience-*feelings* are not based on conscience-knowing, then there is no reason to think they are true. If there is no certainty, there is no basis for certitude. If conscience is more like itching than like reading, more feeling than seeing, then it doesn't even make any sense to talk about truth or falsehood in conscience, any more than to talk about truth or falsehood in itching. And then there can be no such thing as a mistaken conscience, any more than there is a mistaken itch.

This change in our usage of the word "conscience," from knowing to feeling, parallels the change from an objective and absolute morality to a subjective and relative morality, and the silly slogan, "What right do you have to impose *your* (subjective) values (feelings) on others?" Obviously none, *if* values are only feelings, like itches. But suppose they are facts, like icebergs? If the navigator of the Titanic had told the captain to steer away from that iceberg, would he have been "imposing his values on others"?

HOW DO WE KNOW? DIFFERENT KINDS OF KNOWING

One reason why many people think of conscience as feeling rather than knowing is because its kind of knowing is not the kind the modern world is most familiar with: calculative "figuring." Rather, it is intuitive. But people do not realize that intuition too can be *knowing*, not just *feeling*.

When you see something with your senses, your outer eyes, it is immediate, directly present. When you "see" some truth with your inner eye of intuitive knowledge, that is also immediate and directly present. Finally, when you feel something, whether physical, like pain, or spiritual, like joy, it is also immediate and direct. But when you reason and calculate and figure, that is not immediate but mediated, step by step.

Physically *seeing* the moon, intuitively *knowing* that murder is wrong, and *feeling* responsible to pay your debts are all immediate and intuitive. But *reasoning* that since it is unjust to treat the innocent and the guilty the same way, that unborn babies are innocent and convicted murderers are guilty, and therefore it is unjust to treat the babies and the murderers in the same way—this is a matter of reasoning. The conclusion is not *immediately* obvious; that's why it's a matter of argument, why different people have different opinions about it. Not that there is no right and wrong answer to that question. But not everyone sees it, as they see the moon, or the wrongness of murder, or the moral obligation to repay a debt.

We have just distinguished (1) physical seeing, (2) intellectual seeing [intuition], (3) intellectual reasoning, and (4) feeling. Conscience works primarily in area (2), seeing, then areas (3) reasoning, and (4) feeling. The above example of moral reasoning, about abortion and capital punishment, began with something intuitively known: that it is unjust to treat innocent and guilty alike. Then it reasoned from that starting point to a particular conclusion about abortion and capital punishment. Both of these operations of conscience—intuiting and reasoning—were matters of seeing and knowing, not feeling.

Conscience also feels, of course. We feel guilty or innocent, but only because we see something, *e.g.,* that we damaged another person's reputation, and that this was wrong. If we didn't first see those facts, we would not feel those guilt feelings. The seeing spills over into the feeling; but people today tend to confuse the spillover with the source, to reduce conscience to a *mere* matter of feeling.

IS CONSCIENCE A MATTER OF THE WILL?

Does the will also play a role in conscience and its moral discernment process? Not only does it play a role, it plays the central role.

Scripture emphasizes the "heart" as the central power or faculty in us, and this seems to mean something very close to or including the will. Solomon says, in Proverbs, "Keep thy heart with all diligence, for out of it are the issues of life" (Proverbs 4:23, *KJV*). Jesus explicitly singles out the will as the key to discerning the meaning and authority of his teachings, as the key answer to the hermeneutical question, the question of interpretation, which so many scholars worry about and write about today, when he tells the unbelieving Jews who complain that they cannot understand his teaching or accept his authority: "If any man's will is to do his will [God's], he shall know whether the teaching is from God . . ." (John 7:17).

Which comes first, then? Knowing the good or willing it? We seem to have a chicken-and-egg problem here. Each of the two is needed to precede the other. Without a good will, we cannot have good discernment: Jesus tells us that in the passage above. But without discerning what is good, how can we will it?

Plato overemphasized knowledge in morality when he said that knowing the good is all we need, that if we only knew the good, we would always choose it. But he was surely right when he said that a choice without knowledge cannot have moral value. For instance, running at the enemy lines in a blind rage on the battlefield is not an act of moral courage. Without *knowing* the good, we cannot *choose* it.

But the other half of the chicken-and-egg dilemma is equally true: without a good *will* we cannot *understand*— either God, or ourselves, or our neighbors, or true morality, which intimately concerns all three, God and self and neighbor. The way to understand impersonal nature is through impersonal reason, but the way to understand persons, with wills, is through our own personal will's openness.

Which comes first? It is like the senses and the mind: each precedes the other. For the senses to make sense, the mind must interpret and classify what they see. There is no pure, raw, uninterpreted sensation. But for the mind to learn anything, it must gather all its data from the senses. There can be no egg without a chicken and no chicken without an egg.

THE PRACTICAL SOLUTION TO THE CHICKEN AND THE EGG PROBLEM

Perhaps the problem is unsolvable theoretically. But there is a solution practically. Everyone who asks a question about good and evil already has enough knowledge to ask it. Where that knowledge came from is no longer practically important, because the knowledge is already there. The need *now,* the practical need for the present, is to *will* the good.

And that is under our present control. We may not be free to find the truth about some far or obscure thing, but we are always free to choose the good insofar as we know it. The mind has already led the will to its present place, the first need *now* is for the will to act, *then* it will understand and discern. The first thing in the past may have been knowledge of the good, but the first thing in the present must be willing the good.

If we wait until *all* the knowledge of good and evil is in, we will never choose. But if we choose on the basis of the little knowledge we have, we will increase our knowledge. Saints, who choose good, understand both good and evil (for we understand evil only through good, as we understand darkness only through light). The heart has eyes that are opened by exercise.

The eyes of the heart are also the eyes of faith. Faith is fundamentally a choice of the heart, or will. The primary object of faith, Aquinas tells us, is not a doctrine but a person. We accept the teaching with our mind only after we accept the teacher with our will. We believe Christ's teachings only because we first of all believe *him.*

That is why it is just for God to make faith the requirement of salvation. How unjust and irrational it would be to make the difference between Heaven and Hell depend on intellectual knowledge or emotional feelings! But God has made the difference between Heaven and Hell depend on faith. Therefore faith cannot be fundamentally a matter of knowledge or feelings, but of the heart (will).

That's why we are responsible for it: it is our free choice. We learn later that even this free choice to say yes to God was part of God's prior free choice to say yes to us, part of predestination and divine grace. Yet it is truly free and truly ours (for that is precisely *what* God predestined and graced: our free choice).

THE HERMENEUTICS OF THE HEART

The basic principle of the hermeneutics of the heart is that we must interpret the words of a speaker from the standpoint of the speaker's own intentions, *i.e.*, his own heart. It is the most fundamental of all principles of literary criticism, and the one most ignored (for we love to commit the sin of literary pride and interpret the author's words in light of our own heart, intentions, thoughts, and beliefs rather than his). Matthew Arnold formulated the rule this way: we must read an author's words in the same spirit he wrote them. We must share not just his words but his mind. We must abandon our position without and find our position within his mind.

This applies also to God, who is also a speaker, or inspirer of speech, the primary author of Scripture. Therefore we can know God's word rightly only if we know God rightly. "Rightly" means heart to heart, center to center, "deep calling unto deep."

That requires love. Who understands God's law best? The psalmist who sings, "Oh, how I love thy law! It is my meditation all the day" (Psalm 119:97). The lover of God alone understands the law of God, but not either the legalist or the dissenter, because the lover understands it from within, from within the heart and will of God, which neither the external legalist nor the rebel dissenter do. Meanwhile, the legalist and the dissenter both cover up their own lack of love by denouncing the errors of each other.

The Christian has data, just as the scientist does. Discernment will never work if it ignores its data. The Christian's data is divine revelation, "the deposit of faith," *i.e.*, Scripture as continuously and consistently interpreted by the faithful church through history. A "dissenter" can hardly be expected to discern the true spirit of the very data he or she "dissents" from.

SEVEN PRACTICAL PRINCIPLES FOR KNOWING GOD'S WILL

1. The first principle of discernment, then, is "the hermeneutics of the heart." The primary principle of all Christian discernment is embarrassingly simple: love God. If you love God, you will love his will; if you love his will, you will want to do his will; if you want to do his will, you will want to know his will (in order to do it); and if you *want* to know his will, you *will*—according to his own infallible guarantee, straight from the lips of Omniscience. Repeatedly, God incarnate assures us that all who seek, find. Clearly this refers to finding God and his will. Not all who seek glory, or wealth, or even health, will find them; but all who seek God will find him.

But many seem to seek without finding. Wait. You will. God cannot renege on a promise. "God said it, that settles it, and I believe it."

Is this too simple, too childlike for your taste? Please remember who, according to the supreme authority, can enter the Kingdom of Heaven: "Unless you become as little children . . ." God did not inspire the Bible as questions for scholars but as answers for his children.

How will he honor his promise that all seekers find? And when? And will we be conscious of his guidance? Will we feel it? Perhaps so, perhaps not. He has not revealed answers to *those* questions. But even if our feelings are full of doubt and darkness and despair, our faith is our flashlight, not our feelings, and the object of our faith is divinely revealed facts, not humanly generated feelings.

2. A second practical principle of discernment is that we are able to discern God's will and word by the same means it was first revealed: *by the Holy Spirit.* The author is available right now to interpret his book (see John 16:13). The Holy Spirit is not pious rhetoric—unless a powerful windstorm is pious rhetoric (see John 3:8). You cannot see the wind, but you can certainly see the difference it makes.

3. A third principle of discernment concerns obstacles. Why, with such powerful help available, does discernment seem so difficult? Not because there's not enough power there, but because there are too many powers there. There are obstacles that we put in the way. Our third practical principle of discernment is that we must remove the main obstacle to discernment. Every Christian should know what that is. It is *sin.* The major obstacle to *knowing* God's will is *not doing* it.

But the obstacle is not sin as such, but unrepented sin. None of us can avoid all sin. Saints are simply sinners saved. But when sin is unacknowledged and unrepented, it sticks to our spirit and blinds our mind. Repented sin is like garbage put out for the divine garbageman to take away. Unrepented sin is like garbage left in the kitchen that stinks up the air around all the food.

Perhaps there is not a radical increase in sin in our day, but there is certainly a radical increase in unrepented sin. I think humanity has been specializing in sin in every age; different ages only choose different sins to specialize in. Our ancestors were cruel, we are cowardly. They were self-righteous, we are unrighteous. They were full of pride, we are full of lust. I see no simple increase in sin, but I see a radical increase in rationalization of sin, a radical decrease in repentance.

In the Catholic church, the confessional gathers cobwebs. In mainline Protestantism there is fear of anything that might smack of the bad old days of "hell-fire and damnation sermons." Among theologians, labels are blurred: what used to be clearly labeled sin is now labeled maturity, or updating, or adjustment.

Rationalizing sin rather than repenting of it blocks discernment, especially concerning those sins which modernity rationalizes the most, namely sexual sins, because addicts cannot see clearly. The promiscuous very much don't want to see God with a "stop" sign in front of the sin they love more than him. The homosexual very much wants to believe God does not disapprove of his lifestyle. A married person who is in love with someone other than his spouse desperately desires God to approve divorce and remarriage. And so discernment becomes almost impossible. This is not a moralistic sermon but a diagnostic fact. We know it is true not by faith but by experience.

Once our will is out of line with God's, only three things can happen. Either (1) we get in line, turn, repent, and restore the God-relationship and with it the power of discernment; or (2) we keep walking away from God, knowing what we're doing but doing it anyway; or (3) we walk away but rationalize it because we can't endure the truth that we're turning our backs on God, on truth, on the source and standard of all goodness, including our own. Option (1) is not very common today, but option (3) is.

The alternative to both (2) and (3) is (1), repentance. Repentance is threefold: it is a matter of the heart, the mind, and the behavior. It is a matter of the heart because the heart is the captain of the soul. It is a matter of the mind because we must "bring every thought into captivity to Christ." And it is a matter of behavior because "faith without works is dead." The will is the captain, the mind is the navigator, and the hands and feet are the engines of our ship. The whole ship needs to turn (repent).

Repentance necessarily results in changed behavior just as apple trees necessarily result in apples. "Faith without works is dead" means that a faith that does not bear fruit in good works is not a real or living faith in the first place, just as an apple tree that bears no apples is not a real, living apple tree. It's either a dead one or another kind of tree entirely.

4. A fourth practical principle of discernment focuses in on one particular sin that blocks discernment more than any other: unforgiveness. If rationalization instead of repentance is a special danger for the Left, an angry, unforgiving spirit is a special danger for the Right. There are both Sadducees and Pharisees still.

How important is forgiveness? So important that Christ commanded us to mortgage our very salvation on it, when he told us to pray, "Forgive us our trespasses *as we forgive* those who trespass against us." We are told to pray for our own damnation if we do not forgive our neighbors!

Why such an extreme? Because forgiveness is like love: mutual, give and take; so that if we are unforgiving, we must be unforgiven. It's not that God chooses to refuse us his gift of forgiveness to punish us for not forgiving others, but that it is intrinsically impossible for us to be forgiven if we are unforgiving. How could we accept forgiveness from God if our hands are closed like fists refusing to give forgiveness to others? There is simply no place in us for God to deposit his forgiveness if we refuse to open a "forgiveness account." But if we do open such an account, others can draw on it from us. That's the very nature of the account.

Here is a parallel in nature. An unforgiving spirit is like the Dead Sea. It has no outlet. So even the living waters (which are like forgiveness from others) that it receives from the Jordan River turn to dead water when received into the Dead Sea. On the other hand, the Sea of Galilee is alive and full of fish because it has an outlet as well as an inlet. This sea is alive because it passes on the gifts it receives. It is exactly the same with us. If we dam up love's exit river to our neighbor, we also dam up love's entrance river from God.

An unforgiving heart is so at odds with the heart of God, whose very nature is to forgive, that it cannot discern God's will. So before trying to discern God's will, be sure you aren't holding a grudge against anyone. If there is this "root of bitterness" (Hebrews 12:15) in your heart, then for the sake of discernment, but much more, for the sake of your eternal salvation, get down on your knees immediately to ask God's forgiveness for your unforgivingness, and then get up off your knees just as immediately and pass that gift on to your enemy. As Abraham Lincoln said, the way to conquer your enemy is to make him your friend.

5. A fifth principle for discernment is to realize that discernment is a habit, not a quick fix. It grows, gradually, like fruit, like the "fruit of the Spirit." We are so used to instant gratification and technological control today that we find it far more difficult than our ancestors to be patient with nature's (and grace's) slow rhythms of growth. But there can be no mechanical gimmick, no *technique*, for discernment. There may be seven *principles*, but there is no "seven-step *method*" such that if we do x, x will make y happen.

Discernment is a gift from God. There is no "method" for getting a gift. A gift is freely given and freely received.

But discernment is also a habit, and there are methods of cultivating habits. Cultivating habits is like cultivating crops: it takes time. The habit, like the crop, has to grow from within; it is not made from without, like a machine, but the farmer can help it grow.

Habits can fertilize other habits. The habit that most

fertilizes discernment, I think, is "the practice of the presence of God" (to quote Brother Lawrence's classic title).
This is not some mind-game, some "transformation of
consciousness" technique. It is pure and simple realism,
seeing what's really there, living in the real world—unless
God is not real.

We practice the presence of God by faith, not by sight and
not by feeling. The beautiful light in the sky that you see
with your eyes is not God. Neither is the wonderful feeling
you feel in your soul. Both are only God's footprints, God's
gifts, one in the outer world and the other in the inner. The
practice of the presence of God does not mean the attempt to
cultivate a certain kind of permanent feeling. For one thing,
that is impossible. There are no permanent feelings, any
more than there are permanent rainbows. The law of
feelings is the law of undulation. They come like waves and
go like waves. For another thing, even if it *were* possible to
feel God always, we have to learn to focus on God instead of
on ourselves and our feelings. This is equally true when our
feelings are exalted and when they are depressed. Focusing
on God when we feel exalted avoids pride; focusing on God
when we feel depressed avoids despair.

The ancients made idols of things in the physical world,
idols of silver and gold and stone. We may think we have
progressed out of the error of idolatry, but we have not. We
make just as many idols, but in the inner, psychological
world. We make our idols out of happiness and adjustment
and self-acceptance and contentment. To the worshiper of
any idol, any substitute god, objective or subjective, the real
God comes with a shock, like a sword: "Thou shalt have no
other gods before Me!"

If we put other gods before God, they block our practice of
the presence of the real God. And if we do not practice the
presence of God, discerning his will becomes very difficult:
how could you know the will of a stranger? So idolatry is
another sin to single out as a special obstacle to discernment.

Abraham must have practiced the presence of God supremely well. For when God commanded him to offer up his son Isaac as a holocaust, any other man would surely have doubted it was God speaking to him. If God spoke to you tonight and commanded you to sacrifice your son, what would you do? Call a psychiatrist, of course. How could Abraham be so completely sure that this was God speaking to him and not his own unconscious playing tricks on him, or even the Devil deliberately deceiving him? Only because Abraham must have known God better than he knew his own wife.

That is precisely the ideal the saints aim for, and what we hope for in Heaven. That is how Jesus *defined* Heaven, in his high priestly prayer to his Father, in John 17:3: "This is eternal life; that they know thee the only true God. . . ." The closer we get to that knowledge, by the practice of the presence of God, the nearer we get to Heaven and the clearer discernment of God's will becomes.

6. A sixth principle of discernment is the *first* one Augustine or Aquinas would mention, but one we hardly hear about today. It is called prudence.

Prudence is one of the four cardinal virtues. It means practical wisdom. It is a matter of reason, intelligence, and common sense applying principles to practice. This intellectual ingredient in discernment seems to be largely ignored by those who (rightly) emphasize the heart and the Spirit. But that is a disastrous omission. God gave us minds to use, not to file away. He speaks through natural means, and our minds are primary among them.

I began this list of principles by emphasizing the primacy of the heart over the head. But that does not mean the heart works without the head. It's true that knowing God's will is the fruit of willing it, but the medium between willing it and knowing it is usually prudence.

I also emphasized the primacy and need for the Holy

Spirit, as a supernatural source of discernment. But this does not bypass natural reason because "grace does not destroy nature (especially natural reason) but perfects it," in the words of the wise medieval maxim.

More specifically, we must use our minds to discern and discriminate (1) between good and evil; (2) within evil, among the three possible sources of evil, the world, the flesh, and the Devil; and (3) within good, between unchanging principles and changing applications. God did not give us all the answers. He left most of them in our own hands and wits. He gave us a seed packet of principles and trusted us to till the fields of situations with them, water them, and see that they bear good fruit.

There is a real and present danger among many religious people that is the opposite extreme from secularism and is a pendulum-like reaction to it. The secularist seizes the steering wheel of his own life and refuses to let God steer. But religious people often refuse to take the wheel even when God puts it in their hands. It's much more comfortable to cower in a corner and just "let God do it." But to let God's active will into our lives is not to become passive but more active. God's will turns our wills on, not off. And God's mind turns our minds on, not off.

There should be no limit to our submission to God's will; that's true. But one of the things God wills is for us to use our own reason in making specific moral decisions. Therefore to say to God, "You do my thinking for me, please," is *not* submission but rebellion. When you say to God, "Thy will be done," he replies, "My will is for you to use the mind I gave you." Thinking in obedience to God is very different from thinking in disobedience to God or by ignoring God, and both are very different from not thinking at all.

7. A seventh and last principle of discernment is what I shall call spiritual triangulation. Discernment uses a kind of trigonometry, like navigation. If all three factors line up, we can be sure we have discerned rightly; if not, we haven't. It's like lining up three beacon lights to get a triply reinforced illumination, or lining up three dots on a plank to be sure you cut it straight.

The three factors are:

1. God's objective moral law, revealed in Scripture (and, for Catholics, the church's authoritative interpretation of it);

2. the situation God providentially arranges for you;

3. the testimony of your own conscience, especially the inner peace that is a mark of the Spirit's presence.

To discern by objective law alone (1) is legalism. To discern by situations alone (2) is to drift into relativism. To discern by private conscience alone (3) is to drift into subjectivism. To discern by lining up all three is to be wise.

For instance, if your conscience seems to tell you that God wants you to move to another state, but your situation makes this impossible because your responsibilities here won't let you, then your conscience was wrong. Conscience can err, of course. Only God is infallible. Your present situation is part of God's providential control, and part of the data of discernment. It must line up with law and conscience. God opens and closes doors for you.

Or suppose you think God wants you to become a missionary, but you flunk out of Bible school. Or you think God wants you to stay in your business, but it goes bankrupt. Then God is speaking to you through your situation, and showing you that what you thought was God's will was not in fact his will for you.

However, the situation alone is not enough to lead you. Suppose your situation seems to be telling you to divorce and remarry. Suppose your conscience also seems to be telling you this. But God's own Word forbids it, clearly, in all four Gospels, straight from Christ's lips. Then you must seek another situation, not let the situation lead you, and conform your conscience to God's Word, not conform God's infallible Word to your fallible conscience.

Or suppose you read in God's Word that you should feed the poor and your conscience tells you to, but your situation is that you are a poor pastor of a rich congregation. Perhaps you should conclude that God wants you to feed the poor indirectly rather than directly, or symbolically rather than literally, to feed the spiritual poor in your flock with his Word rather than the materially poor with money and food.

In all these examples, the three beacons—God's Word, God's providence, and your conscience—must all line up. Following only one or two of them but not all three leads to errors in discernment.

Finally, suppose you are using all seven of these principles of discernment and still having trouble. You simply don't know what God wants you to do here and now. Don't give up on yourself or God. God is answering you, but his answer for now is: Wait. God will fulfill all his promises, but in his time. He gave us promises, not timetables. He's a lover, not a train.

Patience is the art of waiting. It is not necessarily the art of waiting patiently. Job is a famous example of patience, and of the distinction between patient waiting and waiting patiently. Poor Job cannot discern the meaning of his sufferings. He does not know what he has done (to provoke God to let him suffer so), nor what he can do (to find God or to understand his situation). He searches for thirty-seven agonizing chapters, without finding God, or answers, or comfort. Yet he holds on, and hopes. That is his patience.

I used to think that only those who never read his book could call Job patient. I thought Job was the most *im*patient man in the Bible. But then I realized that the Bible itself calls Job patient (James 5:10-11), so I had to rethink what patience meant. I concluded that it did not necessarily mean a calm emotional state, for Job certainly didn't have that, yet Job had patience, according to James. So patience has to be something deeper than an emotional state.

I think patience is simply waiting, enduring, holding on.

That is all some of us can do. But it is enough. When you can do nothing but hang on and keep trying and losing, or suffering and dying, know that that is something more precious than winning—that is patience.

God had patience with us. He stuck it out with us. He stayed with us, even after we rejected him. It's the least we can do for him when he seems to forsake us, as he seemed to reject Job, because he has promised us that he will never leave us or forsake us, no matter how much our situation seems to tell us that he has. Faith believes God's promises, beyond appearances. Faith holds on, like an anchor, even in the murky depths, even when discernment and light are not possible. Discernment is not always necessary, but faith is.

On the last day, when God calls the rolls, when he gets to your name he will ask, like your old grade school teacher, Present? Are you still here? Are you still with me? If you can honestly answer yes, if you are "present," if you are still seeking the Kingdom of God and his righteousness, then you will have all other things added unto you, including the gift of discernment. All the things you failed to discern during your time on earth, you will discern in the light of eternity. In this life, discernment sheds a little light on the future; in the next life, it will shine Godlight on the past.

THIRTEEN

You Can't Do It
without Power

MORE THAN MORALITY

We come now, finally, to the heart of the problem of morality, which must go beyond morality itself: the power shortage.

There is a lot of good moral advice around, good ideals, good maps. Although our society often refuses to believe them or follow them, the moral maps are there, and have been there for a long, long time. Most of this book is not at all original, but simply traditional. But a car can't run on maps alone; it needs fuel.

It needs maps *too*, and our society has thrown away its maps, its moral dreams. Our society desperately needs a dream, for (in the words of the song from *South Pacific*) "if you don't have a dream, how you gonna have a dream come true?" But even if the dream is restored, even if we dream good moral dreams again, the problem remains: How can we make them real? How do you make the moral dream come true?

Morality drops this problem in our laps, but morality does not solve it. Religion solves it. (I mean by religion a lived relationship with God.) I argued in Chapter Four that you can *know* morality by nature without knowing or believing in religion; that you can know the moral law without knowing its divine source. But though you can *know* morality without knowing religion, you can't *do* it without religion.

Knowledge of our moral duties and our moral failures is only our diagnosis, not our cure. Morality is the diagnosis, religion is the cure. A moralist is only like an x-ray technician; Doctor God is the therapist.

CHRISTIANITY IS FOR FAILURES

A radical difference between mere moral philosophy and Christianity is that moral ideals are for success, but Christianity is for failures. Moral ideals are addressed to people who think they have some hope of attaining those ideals, but Christianity is addressed only to people who have despaired of attaining those ideals by their own power: Christianity comes from Christ, and Christ comes not for "the righteous, but [for] sinners" (Matthew 9:13).

Those who don't know *that* are not yet in the market for Christianity, even though they may sit in church every Sunday. Those who don't know that sit in church as art students would sit in a hospital, enjoying its architecture, but not as its patients. The church is not a museum for saints but a hospital for sinners. To publicly profess to the world that you are a Christian, by going to church every Sunday, is not to say to the world that you are better than they are but that you are desperately ill.

The church is a lot like Alcoholics Anonymous. The very first thing you have to admit and never forget in AA is that "I am an alcoholic." A Christian is one who knows he is a sinaholic, and he has accepted God's cure. The stupidest of all reasons for not going to church is one of the commonest ones: "I'm not good enough." The only qualification is to be *bad* enough. Does anyone refuse to go to the hospital because they're not healthy enough?

NEEDED: TRINITARIAN GRACE

I said above that we can *know* morality by nature but we can *do* it only by divine grace. But we need divine help (grace) even to *know* morality adequately. For not only our moral behavior but also our moral knowledge is critically flawed. Sin has consequences in the mind too. The instrument by which we know morality—conscience—is the voice of God in our soul, yet it is part of our fallen human nature. It is like a heavenly lamp that fell into a polluted sea and got covered over with seaweed. No, it is even more intimately part of our fallen nature than that; it is like a fish swimming through a polluted sea and breathing the pollution in with its gills.

I have spent a lot of time in this book trying to refute moral skepticism and the attitude that morality is always complex and uncertain, never clear and simple. I do not retract any of that. But if we are honest, we must admit that we just don't know very much at all. Oh, we know *something,* and something very real and precious. But it is like a thimbleful of precious water compared to the ocean of truth that is there. How much of what "goodness" really is do you think you really understand? Once we stop fooling ourselves, we will see ourselves not as mariners conquering the seas but as little children on a vast beach with a storm coming up. What we need first and foremost is to put our hand into the hand of our Father.

So we need God's help, God's grace. But divine grace comes to us from the Father only through the Son. So we need not only God the Father but also Christ the Son. A merely transcendent God is not enough. We need a God who loves us enough to come and sit with us in our sickness. We need not just a divine doctor who visits our hospital room now and then, but a human friend who sits beside us. And we have both in the same divine person.

Our sickness is fatal. We need radical surgery. We need salvation, not just moral improvement. The whole human hospital that is our world has been sold by Adam to an evil tyrant called Satan who wants to destroy all the patients. We have been pawned to Satan, and Christ is the only one who can buy us back (that is what "redemption" means), at a terrible price.

Christ is not only the capstone but the foundation of morality. He says, "Without me you can do nothing" (see, for example, John 15:4). Did you get that? Not "without me you can do little, without me you cannot do everything," but "without me you can do nothing—nothing at all." Not "without me you cannot be finished and complete," but "without me you cannot even begin."

For Jesus not only carries out God's treatment to us the patients, but he also prepares us for the doctor. He not only *completes* God's work on us, he also *begins* it. The Mediator mediates both ways: from God to us and from us to God. On the one hand, "No one has ever seen God; the only Son, who is in the bosom of the Father, he has made him known" (John 1:18); on the other hand, "No one comes to the Father but by me" (John 14:6).

We need the Son as well as the Father to be good for the same reason we need the sunlight as well as the sun to be tanned. The sun never stops shining, as God never stops loving; but that's not enough. We need to stay in the sunlight if we are to be tanned, and we need to stay in the Sonlight if we are to be good (see John 15:9-10).

The Spirit is "the missing person" of the Trinity. Most churches ought to file a missing person report on him. But we need him just as we need Jesus: we need Jesus in order to know the Father, and we need the Spirit in order to know Jesus. "No one can say 'Jesus is Lord!' except by the Holy Spirit" (1 Corinthians 12:3).

The Father is God above us, the Son is God beside us, the Spirit is God within us. We need all three persons, for we need to be immersed and baptized in God's grace totally (since we are totally needy), inside, outside, inside out and upside down.

Thousands, even millions of Christians today know from their own experience what an enormous difference being baptized in the Holy Spirit has made to their lives: the differences between knowing God only outside and knowing him also inside, between knowing *of* him and knowing *him*; the difference between a picture and a person, a blueprint and a building, between reading a ghost story and being haunted. Being baptized in the Spirit does not bring magical, instant perfection. But the Spirit does bring a new intimacy, a touching, an insideness. God becomes a spring of living water welling up from within, just as Jesus promised (John 4:14; 7:37-39), rather than only a bright light from above.

I think it is largely the lack of this intimacy in the lives of most Christians that leads them into the cults, the New Age movement, and Oriental religions, all of which offer this experiential, personal, subjective dimension, but without the objective truth. The answer to such false or incomplete religions is not merely *true* religion (orthodoxy) but also *complete* religion; truth within as well as truth without. Orthodoxy alone is not enough, as a map is not enough. We need the ability to follow the map. That's why we need the Spirit.

SEVEN POWER AIDS

Here are seven power aids, all associated with the Holy Spirit's work, which we need in our spiritual warfare. Each of them comes from the Spirit and leads to greater intimacy and life in the Spirit.

The first power aid is *prayer.* Prayer is power. Prayer is touching the human wire to the divine dynamo. "More things are wrought by prayer than this world dreams of" (Tennyson).

There have been millions of pages of advice about prayer. Instead of repeating any of them here, I want to say just two little words, which are more important than all those millions of pages, however true they are. The words are: DO IT!

We need to know *how* to pray, of course, but for most of us the problem comes before that, on a much simpler level: even more than learning how to do it, we need to actually do it. Just do it. Just say yes. If we won't give God fifteen minutes of totally uninterrupted prayer of *any* kind each day, then all the books in the world on how to pray will not help us much.

The second power aid is *familiarity with God's Word,* the Bible. Jesus says that the secret of power in prayer is that his words are to "abide" or "dwell" in us (John 15:7). Since God's Word is powerful and alive (Hebrews 4:12), therefore if it lives within us we will have not only truth but also power. We must not simply know God's Word as a student knows a textbook on an exam; we must know it as we know our own body or our own house. We must live in it. When God's Word becomes the air our spirit breathes, we will begin to fly like an eagle (see Isaiah 40:31).

The Bible uses the same phrase, "the Word of God," to refer both to the Bible and to Jesus. Both are the pure and infallible revelation of the mind of the Father, one in print and the other in flesh. The two are related like a portrait and a person. The Bible is a portrait of Christ. Every word in the book is a picture of some wrinkle or pore in his flesh. The two reinforce each other: the more we love and understand him, the more we will love and understand his portrait, and the more we love and understand his portrait, the more we will love and understand him.

One of the sharpest differences being baptized in the Holy Spirit makes is in our understanding of Scripture. When the primary author of Scripture is within us, lighting up our minds *and* lighting up the page, then the light within and the light without meet like two beams of light becoming one. When Scripture thus newly lights up for us under the power of the Spirit, it is like reading letters from a person who used to be a stranger but now is a close friend. Of course you understand his words better now; you understand from within, not without.

A third power aid is the Christian *community.* Other people help us to be either good or evil. The visible and invisible community called the church has many aspects and many functions, but here is an embarrassingly simple one that we tend to forget: it helps us to be good.

We need each other. Do-it-yourself sanctity is a self-contradiction. Cut a table into four parts and no one of the parts will stand up. But when each leg of the table leans against the others, it stands. It is the same with us. The table is the church and each of us is a leg. The church is a body, and each of us is an organ. (It's all in 1 Corinthians 12.) This principle too is well known and used by Alcoholics Anonymous. The church is similar: it is the community of Sinners Anonymous.

The fourth power aid is *silence.* This goes with the previous one, community, even though most of us have a natural tendency to prefer either one of the two to the neglect of the other. We need both community and silence, both dialog and solitude. For without silence, community becomes shallow noise, and without community, silence becomes dangerously self-centered.

We can learn both the *need* for silence and some *methods* of cultivating it from Oriental religions (Hinduism, Buddhism, and Taoism). But we can learn the same two things more surely and securely from our own saints and mystics. The danger of turning to Oriental religions for techniques is that those techniques usually cultivate silence for its own sake, as a kind of objectless self-hypnosis, rather than as a means to the greater end of love of God and neighbor. Oriental religions are profoundly aware of our need for silence and detachment and contemplation, as our modern world is not. But these religions are usually *not* aware also of the greater end of love. Oriental religions do not know a God with a will and a law and love, only a God of "pure *consciousness.*" Oriental techniques of prayer are only for purifying our consciousness, not for sanctifying our will. Mysticism is their ultimate ideal; sanctity is ours. The two can aid each other, but they are not the same.

I think the average Christian's most immediate and pressing danger is *not* the danger of sailing too close to the Oriental shore of silence-for-the-sake-of-silence, but the danger of sailing too far away from it toward the shore of modern Western worldliness, busyness, noisiness, hastiness, and superficiality. (See Chapter Ten on simplicity.) The East prays inadequately, but the West prays hardly at all.

And we cannot pray without silence. We cannot hear God's Word, within or even without, without silence. We cannot hear the Spirit interpret to us the Word without silence and listening. We cannot hear the word of God in our conscience without silence.

We cannot be good without silence. For without silence we cannot grow deep roots, and without deep roots we cannot develop character, and without character we cannot be good.

A fifth power aid is *joy.* "The joy of the Lord is your strength" (Nehemiah 8:10). Joy is not just happiness and satisfaction, but dynamism, movement, strength to win the world. Joy is not just fulfillment, an ending of a quest, but it is power and strength, a beginning.

The world thinks Christians are gloomy and deadly serious people. That wonderfully joyful Christian, G.K. Chesterton, wrote that "the only unanswerable argument against Christianity is Christians" (*i.e.*, joyless Christians). The world looks at us and says, "Whatever they've got, I don't want it."

But the world looked at the early Christians and said, "Whatever they've got, I want it." That's how twelve fishermen conquered the world. The world saw a secret joy there and had to find out what made men go to the lions with hymns on their lips.

The Catholic church will not canonize a saint, publicly declaring his life to be a model worthy of imitation, unless a number of strict qualifications are met, and one of them is joy. Joyless saints are a contradiction in terms. For joy is the second gift of the Holy Spirit, after love (see Galatians 5:22-23).

A sixth power aid is *suffering.* Suffering is not the opposite of joy. On the contrary, Christian joy is made perfect through suffering, and Christian suffering is the highest joy. It may be difficult for us to understand or accept that, but all the saints say it. Their greatest joy is to suffer for Christ. The explanation, the link between these two apparently opposite things, is, of course, love.

Sometimes, all we can do is suffer. Sometimes we have tried everything else and failed, and have no hope left. But there is always one thing we can do: we can always suffer. An old, hopelessly ill, bedridden and paralyzed patient in a nursing home may be one of the most powerful people in the world in the eyes of God, *i.e.*, in truth.

For a Christian never suffers alone, but in Christ, with Christ, as part of Christ's body. The suffering Christ endured in his body on the cross, and still endures in his body the church throughout the world, is the greatest power the world has ever seen. Calvary turned the whole world into a cross; any Christian can plug into that same power (Colossians 1:24).

The most powerful thing Christ did was not his miracles but his suffering. One of his miracles of healing won health for one person, but one drop of his blood in death won

Heaven for millions. Our power, like that of Jesus, our head, is "made perfect in weakness" (2 Corinthians 12:9) and suffering.

The seventh power aid is illustrated by the example of the Virgin Mary, who according to Scripture was "well favored," "blessed among women," and "full of grace." She modeled for us three great secrets of spiritual power: pondering, positivity, and praise.

Mary had the habit of "pondering [all these things] in her heart" (Luke 2:19). She was a true contemplative.

Mary was totally ready to say to God with her whole heart the positive word yes, "Let it be to me according to your word" (Luke 1:38). That is the simple secret of all sanctity.

Mary's sanctity was perfected in praise. Her "Magnificat" (Luke 1:46-55) is perfect Christian praise. This is a secret of power. As Merlin Carothers' profound title (and profound book) puts it, there is "power in praise."

The three go together and in order. Pondering gives depth to our lives, prepares our spiritual womb for God's coming. Positivity lets God in. And praise lets the light shine out.

PROGNOSIS

Empowered by the Spirit and by these seven power-aids, we can win the world for Christ again. Goodness is winsome. Goodness elicits hatred from some, but it elicits love and emulation from many. It is infectious. One Mother Teresa has won more hearts than a million books.

My point is not merely that we should be optimistic about winning individual *souls.* That is true at all times. My point is that we should be optimistic about winning the *world,* re-Christianizing this de-Christianized, apostate world. The West is old and tired, a ripe fruit ready to fall off the branch into our hands. We are no longer the old establishment but the new rebels, the wave of the future. To a world that has tried everything and found it vanity, orthodoxy is the only possible novelty for tomorrow.

Our testimony will win the world only if it is complete, and to be complete, it must be two-pronged, or two-bladed, like a scissors: in words and in deeds. The words must have real deeds behind them, because deeds are data for words to be *about*. The early Christians won the world not only by words but by deeds, by *doing* the truth as well as *telling* the truth. We must do the same.

I began this book with a pessimistic diagnosis of our modern world, and that diagnosis has continued in every chapter. Yet, without retracting any of that, I am optimistic, for all the prophets were too. They, too, said many pessimistic things, many offensively negative things. But they were ultimately optimistic and hopeful. In fact, they always stretched our thinking in *two* directions farther than we would go ourselves, because they told us how God sees us, and God sees us as walking a road to one or the other of *two* destinies—eternal bliss or eternal misery—that it is clearly worth anything and everything in the world, anything and everything in our lives, to attain the one and escape the other.

Here is how a modern prophet expressed this perennial Christian vision of the meaning of our lives and the incalculable importance of making choices. It is, I think, the greatest passage written by the greatest Christian writer of our century, the conclusion of C.S. Lewis' sermon entitled (appropriately) "The Weight of Glory":

It is a serious thing to live in a society of possible gods and goddesses, to remember that the dullest and most uninteresting person you can talk to may one day be a creature which, if you saw it now, you would be strongly tempted to worship, or else a horror and a corruption such as you now meet, if at all, only in a nightmare. All day long we are, in some degree, helping each other to one or other of these destinations. It is in the light of those overwhelming possibilities, it is with the awe and circumspection proper to them, that we should conduct all our dealings with one another, all friendships, all loves, all play, all politics. There are no *ordinary* people. You have never talked to a mere mortal. Nations, cultures, arts, civilizations—these are mortal, and their life is to ours as the life of a gnat. But it is immortals whom we joke with, work with, marry, snub, and exploit—immortal horrors or everlasting splendours.

That is the issue ultimately at stake in making choices.

Other Books of Interest from Servant Publications

Knowing the Truth of God's Love
by Peter Kreeft

With unusual clarity, Peter Kreeft points out that the man or woman who begins to glimpse the God who is Creator, Redeemer, and Lover of our souls will never be the same. He describes Scripture as a love story and then tells why divine love answers our deepest problems. Posing the hard questions about love that rankle the heart, Peter Kreeft never settles for easy answers. Instead, he exposes today's superficial attitudes about love in order to lead people to a deeper understanding of what it means to be loved by God. *$8.95*

Making Sense Out of Suffering
by Peter Kreeft

This account of a real honest personal quest is both engaging and convincing. (Peter Kreeft records his own wrestling match with God as he struggles to make sense out of pain and suffering.) It delights as well as informs. Written from a deep well of wisdom derived from experience and careful observation, *Making Sense Out of Suffering* is a book for empty hearts, not full ones. Read it if you are hungry for insight into the mystery of suffering. *$6.95*

Available at your Christian bookstore or from:
Servant Publications • Dept. 209 • P.O. Box 7455
Ann Arbor, Michigan 48107
Please include payment plus $1.25 per book
for postage and handling.
*Send for our FREE catalog of Christian
books, music, and cassettes.*